LAUG   G
GAS

edited by

Michael Sheldin &
David Wallechinsky
with
Saunie Salyer

RONIN Publishing, Inc.   Berkeley California

Laughing Gas

Copyright 1973, 1992 by Michael Sheldin, David Wallechinsky & Saunie Salyer
Pbook Isbn: 978-0-914171-52-2
Ebook ISBN: 978-1-57951-266-8

Published by
RONIN Publishing, Inc.
Po Box 3436
Oakland CA 94609
www.roninpub.com

Distributed to the trade by **Publishers Group West**/Ingram
Printed in the United States of America by **Lightning Source**

<u>Notice to Reader</u>

A GRAND
EXHIBITION

OF THE EFFECTS PRODUCED BY INHALING

NITROUS OXIDE, EXHILERATING, OR

LAUGHING GAS!

WILL BE GIVEN AT *the Masonic Hall*

Saturday **EVENING,** *15th* **1845.**

50 **GALLONS OF GAS will be prepared and adminis- tered to all in the audience who desire to inhale it.**

MEN will be invited from the audience, to protect those under the influence of the Gas from in- juring themselves or others. This course is adopted that no apprehension of danger may be entertained. Probably no one will attempt to fight.

THE EFFECT OF THE GAS is to make those who inhale it, either

LAUGH, SING, DANCE, SPEAK OR FIGHT, &c. &c.

according to the leading trait of their character. They seem to retain consciousness enough not to say or do that which they would have occasion to regret.

N. B. The Gas will be administered only to gentle- men of the first respectability. The object is to make the entertainment in every respect, a genteel affair.

These who inhale the Gas once, are always anxious to inhale it the second time. There is not an exception to this rule.

No language can describe the delightful sensation produced. Robert Southey, (poet) once said that " the atmosphere of the highest of all possible heavens must be composed of this Gas."

For a full account of the effect produced upon some of the most distinguished men of Europe, see Hooper's Medical Dictionary, under the head of Nitrogen.

Introduction

by David Presti, Ph.D. and Ross West

Nitrous oxide (N_2O) is an amazing molecule. When compared to other psychoactive compounds – such as LSD, psilocybin, mescaline, and MDMA – which have relatively complex molecular structures consisting of many atoms, the N_2O molecule is remarkable for its three-atom simplicity. Though the mechanism of how nitrous oxide affects the human brain at the cellular and molecular levels is poorly understood, the effects themselves have been thoroughly examined. Nitrous oxide (also called laughing gas) is known to produce states of analgesia (relief from pain) and anesthesia (loss of bodily sensation), properties which have fostered its longtime use as a surgical anesthetic. More to the point of this book, the versatile gas can also bring about states of profoundly altered consciousness.

The discovery of N_2O is generally attributed to Joseph Priestley, scientist, clergyman, religious scholar, and political liberal, who in 1772 reported the isolation of a mixture of nitrogen oxides (including N_2O) which he christened "Dephlogisticated Nitrous Air." Around the same time, the sagacious Priestley, no slouch in the laboratory, also discovered oxygen, nitrogen and ammonia – and an effective way of producing carbonated water by dissolving carbon-dioxide gas in water. Although a golden age of research into gasses was at hand and Priestley was playing an important role in the history of science, his neighbors failed to honor their local luminary. Angry over his political leanings, they formed a mob and burned down his house, his church, and his laboratory in 1791, forcing him to flee the vicinity and later to depart England for America.

But even a mob's torches could not frighten the genie back into the lamp. Less than a decade passed before the Pneumatic Institution, a small medical facility, was established in Bristol,

England. Here, research into the mind-altering qualities of nitrous oxide was first conducted by a group of pioneering self-experimenters under the leadership of physician, scientist, and poet Thomas Beddoes. His colleagues included Humphrey Davy (a brilliant young chemist, who would go on to discover the elements of sodium, potassium, and boron) and Davy's friend Peter Mark Roget (a young physician who, years later, would compile the still-famous *Roget's Thesaurus*).

These were the days of so-called pneumatic medicine – the experimental treatment of various ailments by the inhalation of gasses – and the Pneumatic Institution was at this discipline's center. The Institution also became a kind of Mecca for inner-adventurers, who, keep in mind, were living in a time and place where opium was generally available from the local apothecary as an over-the-counter medicine. Davy found that, when measured against "high intoxication from opium or alcohol," nitrous oxide could produce "an excitement equal in duration and superior in intensity."

A careful observer, Davy was the first to appreciate the analgesic properties of nitrous oxide. Between working with the "patients" who came to the Institution to be treated and heavily dosing themselves, the Institution staff compiled a wealth of data on the effects of nitrous oxide that remains of interest today. Many of these observations were brought together by Davy in a 580-page treatise (*Researches, Chemical and Philosophical; Chiefly Concerning Nitrous Oxide, or Dephlogisticated Nitrous Air, and its Respiration*) which he published in 1800 at the age of 21. This immediately established his reputation in the scientific community and he was invited to lecture at the Royal Institution in London. Three years later he was elected a Fellow of the prestigious Royal Society.

In the next major scene in the nitrous-oxide drama, the actors are no longer the intellectual elite of England. Enter instead the side-show entertainers and itinerant lecturers who traveled the American landscape in the 1840s. Their performances demonstrated the wonders of the intoxicant that had come to be called "laughing gas," because those who inhaled it frequently became uninhibited and jovial. A handbill for such an exhibition is reproduced as a frontispiece to this book – one can hardly read it without hearing the huckster-incarnate voice of W.C. Fields imploring hayseeds and suckers to "step right up."

Among the checkered group of entertainer-educators who traveled the snake-oil circuit was Gardner Q. Colton. During one of Colton's performances, a volunteer inhaled a quantity of the gas, began to gyrate, then vigorously rammed his shin into a heavy piece of furniture. Seemingly unaware of the damage done, the dancer continued romping about the stage until, as normal consciousness returned, he became painfully aware of his throbbing leg. Watching this scene from the audience was a young man named Horace Wells. It was a fortuitous observation, but "chance favors the prepared mind", as Louis Pasteur would later articulate. As a dentist in the medically primitive days of the 19th century, Wells was only too familiar with pain. The prospect of helping his patients undergo tooth extractions and other harrowing procedures with less agony spurred Wells to successfully experiment, assisted by Colton, with nitrous-oxide-aided dentistry. Wells thus became a pioneer of surgical anesthesia.

Unfortunately, Wells' success was short-lived and his promising life soon slid to hell on greased rails. He became a regular abuser of nitrous oxide, and then moved on to ether and chloroform. Finally, after a chloroform-addled attack on some prostitutes, he was jailed and shortly thereafter committed suicide.

His former partner fared much better, however. As an old side-show man, Colton knew a good thing when he saw it, and the memories of watching Wells perform relatively painless, gas-aided surgeries had never left him. In the 1860s he returned to the game of anesthesiology, and with the help of the gas and a partner, went on to perform thousands of tooth extractions.

Today, one hundred and thirty years later, nitrous oxide remains a commonly used dental anesthetic.

* * * * *

The nitrous-oxide state, in addition to the analgesic and anesthetic properties so useful in dentistry and surgical medicine, has qualities in common with psychedelic states. As is embodied in the word itself (psychedelic means "mind manifesting"), these states are characterized by an increased depth, intensity, and expansion of thought and feeling. Although progress has been made in the description of the tranquilization, anesthesia, analgesia, stimulation, and euphoria brought on by various psychoactive chemicals, the altered states induced by *psychedelic* molecules remain poorly characterized. In fact, the scientific literature has little to say about these properties of nitrous oxide. This is not to say, however, that these properties have been completely overlooked.

The writings of the pioneer psychologist, philosopher, and physician William James still stand prominently in this area. James appreciated, from his own experiments, the power of the unusual altered state of consciousness induced by the gas. He first described his experiences in conjunction with a paper on the philosophy of Hegel, published in the journal *Mind* in 1882. In attempting to make sense of Hegel's ideas, James struggled with the German philosopher's claim that opposites can be united in a "higher synthesis." In his lengthy and thoughtful *Mind* article, James arrived at the conclusion that he could not be a Hegelian because the idea of unification of opposites was to him an irresolvable conundrum, comparable to having one's cake and eating it too.

After completing his article, James was introduced to nitrous oxide. Under its influence, he experienced insights into Hegel's philosophy which led him to compose a short note (reprinted in this book) which appeared as an addendum to his article in *Mind*. There he wrote how the gas had helped him realize that "there are no differences but differences of degree between different degrees of difference and no difference." His rhapsodizing didn't stop there. Some of his other gas-induced exclamations included: "good and evil reconciled in a laugh!" and "sober, drunk, all the same!" Clearly, nitrous oxide had allowed James to glimpse the notion, central to Buddhist and Taoist philosophy, as well as a component of Hegel's, that contradictory notions could indeed be simultaneously acceptable. Forty-some years later, the same notion would emerge as an important aspect of modern physics in the theory of quantum mechanics.

James referred again to his experiences with nitrous oxide in his classic work *The Varieties of Religious Experience*, the text of the Gifford Lectures on Natural Philosophy and Religion delivered to the University of Edinburgh in 1901-1902 – a lectureship which continues to this day to attract great thinkers in the tradition of natural philosophy.

> One conclusion was forced upon my mind at the time [of inhaling nitrous oxide], and my impression of its truth has since remained unshaken. It is that our normal waking consciousness, rational consciousness as we call it, is but one special type of consciousness, while all about it, parted from it by the filmiest of screens, there lie potential forms of consciousness entirely different. We may go through life without suspecting their existence; but apply the requisite stimulus, and at a touch they are there in all their completeness, definite types of mentality which probably somewhere have their application and adaptation. No account of the universe in its totality can be final which leaves these other forms of consciousness quite disregarded. How to regard them is the question....

Nearly a century later, we continue to wrestle with this question of how to regard certain altered states of consciousness. The debate is unarguably complex and is made even more difficult because the very description of the states in question has proven a daunting task. Indeed, one of the frequently mentioned characteristics of altered states of the mystical stripe (which, it is contended, nitrous oxide can induce) is *ineffability*. A large percentage of psychedelic travellers claim that language is inadequate to communicate the experiences through which they journey.

This claim was reconfirmed by the intrepid members of the East Bay Chemical Philosophy Symposium (EBCPS), modern bearers of the torch ignited by Davy, who, in the present book, report on their extensive experience with nitrous oxide. One

EBCPS member commented: "We've taken tape recorders into rooms and tried to speak into them and free associate and tell what was coming into our heads on gas and we found it couldn't be verbalized."

Nearly two centuries ago, Peter Roget articulated his experience by saying: "My ideas succeeded one another with extreme rapidity, thoughts rushed like a torrent through my mind, as if their velocity had been suddenly accelerated by the bursting of a barrier which had before retained them in their natural and equable course."

Humphrey Davy described the effects of one gas-guzzling session this way: "I lost all connection with external things; trains of vivid visible images rapidly passed through my mind, and were connected with words in such a manner as to produce perceptions perfectly novel. I existed in a world of newly connected and newly modified ideas."

James characterizes the central attraction of the gas as follows: "With me, as with every person of whom I have heard, the keynote of the experience is the tremendously exciting sense of an intense metaphysical illumination. Truth lies open to the view in depth beneath depth of almost blinding evidence. The mind sees all the logical relations of being with an apparent subtlety and instantaneity to which its normal consciousness offers no parallel."

The sharp-minded reader may note that for all the dizzying verbiage and fanfare, the experience remains vaguely described. What was so amazing about it? What were these perfectly novel perceptions, these newly connected ideas, these blinding meta-physical insights? And why don't the writers let us in on them?

James explains the difficulty as a curious function of the gas experience itself: "as sobriety returns, the feeling of insight fades and one is left staring vacantly at a few disjointed words and phrases [written during the intoxication], as one stares at a cadaverous-looking snowpeak from which the sunset glow has just fled, or at the black cinder left by the extinguished brand."

The insights made available by the gas are "truths that lie open in depth beneath depth of almost blinding evidence" and moments later "disjointed words and phrases." Surely this is the most perplexing, maddening, and paradoxical aspect of the nitrous-oxide experience. What are we to make, for example, of this lightening bolt of insight, penned by James under the influence of laughing gas: "By George, nothing but othing!"

It seems that the characteristic ineffability of altered states in general is further complicated for nitrous oxide by an apparent inability, in many cases, for users to remember insights gained under its influence. *Transience* is again and again reported as a prominent feature of the experience. It is as if the gas helps to pull back that filmiest of screens, but only for a moment, and at a cost of at least partial amnesia.

These extraordinary states of consciousness provide a rich and fascinating area for scientific study. Within the world of the known psychedelic compounds and their effects (aspects of the N_2O experience here included) lies a wealth of information about the neurochemistry of processes which underlie some of the most magnificent aspects of the human brain: psychological defense mechanisms, attentional processes, memory, and creativity among them. And while we work to understand how more chemically complex psychoactive compounds might interact with neurotransmitter-receptor systems by virtue of molecular similarity with brain neurotransmitters, N_2O remains a puzzle. Does it interact with a specific neurotransmitter receptor? Does it interact with other, non-receptor components of the nervous system, such as membranes or intracellular, second-messenger systems? Does it have a widespread effect on many receptors, by virtue of its being some sort of small and versatile "master key"? In so many ways the brain remains a black box of mysterious chemistry, and psychoactive compounds may contribute to valuable additions to the understanding of the riches and mysteries – neurochemical and psychological – within us all.

* * * * *

Lest one think that every inhalation of N_2O produces a mind-expanding, psychedelic-like altered state, reports by some individuals emphasize merely a feeling of faintness. Others stress the rapid onset ("rush") of numbed consciousness, and some refer predominantly to a throbbing enhancement of auditory perception – making listening to Led Zeppelin, perhaps, a "superheavy vibratory" experience.

Contemporary recreational users of nitrous oxide generally obtain the gas in one of a few ways. Tanks of N_2O occasionally get diverted from supply warehouses, hospitals, and dental offices into the homes of recreational users. Another widespread commercial use of nitrous oxide is as propellant for whipping cream. Small quantities of the gas can be obtained from cans of whipped cream sold in grocery stores. Cartridges of N_2O, called whippets and manufactured for use in pressurizing whipped cream dispensers used by restaurants, are another frequent source of nitrous oxide for recreational use. The user inhales the gas from a balloon inflated with the contents of the cartridge.

Occasionally, following in the footsteps of Priestley and Davy, individuals attempt to synthesize N_2O. This is definitely not recommended, for several reasons. First, the synthetic process frequently employed (heating ammonium nitrate) may lead to an explosion, and has been the cause of major accidents and numerous injuries in the industrial synthesis of N_2O. Second, other oxides of nitrogen may be obtained as byproducts of the synthetic process. One of these, nitrogen dioxide, is extremely toxic, and can lead to rapid destruction of lung tissue, even if inhaled in small quantities.

When the first edition of this book was printed in 1973, laughing gas seemed almost miraculous in its ability to drastically alter consciousness while inflicting on the user virtually no deleterious side effects. Although recreational users sometimes suffocate themselves by failing to breathe adequate amounts of oxygen along with the nitrous oxide, it has been widely believed that when used with sufficient oxygen, nitrous oxide is safe and harmless.

However, beginning in the late 1970s, evidence has been gathered that tempers this benign assessment, for use of nitrous oxide can give rise to several potentially serious problems. The major potential medical complication associated with whiffing laughing gas is known as peripheral neuropathy, the degeneration of nerve fibers controlling sensation and movement in the arms and legs. The first symptom of this kind of trouble is generally a persistent tingling and/or numbness in the fingers and toes, which sometimes develops into a disorder severe enough to require assistance when walking. Other problems associated with prolonged nitrous-oxide use include impotence, impairments of memory and other aspects of mental functioning, and decreased ability of bone marrow to produce white blood cells. These toxic effects have led to the questioning of the widespread use of nitrous oxide as a surgical and dental anesthetic. Although many of the reported cases of neuropathy have involved individuals who had inhaled N_2O many times over periods of several years, some cases occurred after as little as three months of one-to-two recreational inhalations per week. While most of these persons gradually recovered after use was terminated, it also appears that some of the nerve damage suffered may be permanent.

Interestingly, Humphrey Davy had noted that heavy consumption of nitrous oxide produced in him symptoms of distorted sensibility in his fingers, as well as difficulties with sleep, concentration, and mood. He also found that the gas could lead to a kind of psychological dependence; that is, a desire to use the gas was frequently triggered in him by the mere sight of another person breathing it, or even by the sight of the associated 18th-century paraphernalia involved in N_2O use.

Thus we are reminded that one aspect of chemicals which alter consciousness is their potential for abuse, that is, continued use despite adverse effects on one's life. In addition to serious side-effects such as neuropathy, any substance which alters consciousness in a way that relieves anxiety or otherwise increases pleasure carries with it, *ipso facto*, the potential for overuse. Psychoactive substances are best respected for the powerful effects they may have on both the psyche *and* the physiology of users. With nitrous oxide, as with other drugs, education concerning these effects is key.

Deleterious side-effects notwithstanding, there will always be self-experimenters who choose to "Just Say N_2O" rather than "Just Say NO." Indeed, reports by such individuals contribute to our understanding of the effects of nitrous oxide on the human nervous system, complementing laboratory investigations of the physiological and neurochemical effects.

And thus it is that books like this one make an important contribution. It is disturbing, then, that we are living at a time in which new laws and new interpretations of old laws are posing a threat to the availability of such writings. We once had a brush with this sort of censorship in obtaining an earlier edition of *Laughing Gas – Nitrous Oxide*. We had seen the book in the small, but usually well-stocked, "Drugs" section of a favorite second-hand book store, but had passed over purchasing it. Several weeks later, we returned to the store, hoping to obtain the book, as the idea that it was an out-of-print classic had finally percolated into consciousness. However, not only was the book no longer there, but the entire "Drugs" section had disappeared. Puzzled, we approached the store's owner, who indicated that with the recent introduction of a more restrictive drug-paraphernalia law, she had pulled all the books on recreational drug use from the shelves, out of fear of being busted under some global interpretation of the law. Fortunately, the book still remained in the back room, and we were able to purchase it.

With unrestricted reading threatened in this way, the role of And/Or Press in keeping books like this one in print becomes an increasingly valuable one.

Laughing Gas

(Nitrous Oxide)

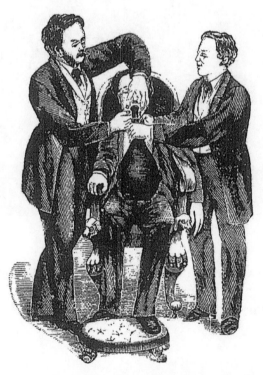

Early method of administering Nitrous oxide

David Wallechinski, Saunie Salyer and Michael Shedlin
(from top to bottom)
circa 1973, time of publication of the first edition of *Laughing Gas*

TABLE OF CONTENTS

THE EFFECTS OF NITROUS OXIDE   A PERSONAL ACCOUNT

T. J. LOGAN

I first inhaled laughing gas on the 16th of August, 1968, while visiting some friends in Berkeley. The couple at whose home I was staying extolled the virtues of the gas for hours in an attempt to overcome my reluctance to take anything chemical into my body. Finally I agreed to try it and my friends put me on a bed between stereo headphones and the sound of Cream playing "Spoonful". Before trying the gas I had been thinking about the fact that every time I tried a new drug, the change of consciousness scared me at first and made me worry that I wouldn't come down. But I always came down.

For a few seconds after my first lungful, I thought that the laughing gas wasn't going to effect me. Then I felt a tremendous rush, a tremendous change, and I quickly reached my self-doubt stage. I tried to make things negative, but I couldn't. By the time I realized this, the effects of the gas were already wearing off and I delighted in the revelation that my fears and bummers were self-caused and didn't have to happen. I had already understood this intellectually, but feeling it was an entirely different experience. I realized that the only reason I would be turned off by nitrous oxide and, by extension, life, would be by clinging insecurely to my traditional conditioning.

Having gone through all this after the first inhalation, I was free to settle back and enjoy my second and third inhalations. I concentrated on the sound of Cream and found that it became sounds of Cream. Each instrument became clear to me (I had never experienced this before) and at one point I found myself in awe of the beauty of a single note.

Trying it without music, I found that my friends' voices reverberated when they spoke to me and instead of worrying about this, I enjoyed it. The evening's experience exhilarated me well into the next day and despite the bad moods and tensions of other people who I encountered, all that I could express was happiness and tolerance. A big step had been made in clearing my mind of irrational worries.

I inhaled laughing gas thrice more the following month and each time felt that I had had the happiest experience of my life. I wanted to turn on everyone I knew and everyone I met, but my supply was limited and I was afraid that giving someone just one hit would frustrate them. I decided that if gas was actually harmless, I would like an ever-ready supply.

It was six months before I had the opportunity (the door to unity) to take gas again. Each hit I took was a new level of awareness in the direction of Buddhist unity. I felt true happiness and envisioned taking it until I died because the nitrous oxide high was what is supposed to be done with life. After breathing several lungsful in a row, I lay back in deep thought, transcendence of experience being my thought for the day. That night I wrote:

> *Nitrous oxide:*
> *a euphoric inspiration*
> *for transcendence of self and experience.*
> *When even the so important difference*
> *between present*
> *and past and future disappears*
> *as all dualisms do.*
> *With gas*
> *reality regains the meaning of*
> *whatever exists*
> *instead of*
> *whatever we are used to.*
> *And death becomes immaterial to life.*
>
> *Nitrous oxide:*
> *ultimate hedonism attained without hard work.*

And I added, in answer to my natural self, "But that is impossible, happiness is a privilege not a right. It comes from work not welfare."

A few days later, from my diary: "Shining through the mediocre, exhausting experiences of the day was a period of great joy. More gas. More and more better. All sorts of spiritual flashes, experienced positively. Specific memory of the experience fades quickly, but I do remember 'incredible'. I remember thinking that I never felt happier." I was afraid to tell people that I was willing to die if that was what followed euphoria.

For months I had been planning to make an experimental movie which would be an improvised documentary. All I had planned for certain was to gather a mixed group of people in a house and film them over a period of days. When the time came to shoot the film I decided to film the "actors" inhaling laughing gas. I was partly motivated by the ice-breaking qualities of nitrous oxide, partly by the fact that I so enjoyed turning people on to gas and partly by my desire to have something definite to film. For the first time, my friends and I obtained a large tank of nitrous oxide which allowed us to remain under the influence for minutes at a time by providing a constant source. We attached a length of garden hose to the valve opening for easier inhaling.

2

Although the crux of the film had nothing to do with drugs, the laughing gas developed into such a major character that the film was eventually titled *Gas*. In addition, the film can only be fully appreciated by an audience that is breathing laughing gas at the same time as the people in the film.

The day following the last day of filming, after a long morning of errands, a friend and I took turns taking gas for ten or fifteen minutes at a time. My first turn I listened to "Spoonful" again and, as usual, had an absolutely beautiful experience. At times my mind switched from the music to thoughts. I kept transcending an entire level of thinking and then finding that the new level was only a small part of a larger level which I would then transcend. Or that all the levels that I had transcended were really one grander scale level which I would then transcend. So much that I was learning from my gas experiences was indescribable and could be communicated only by unpremeditated vibrations.

My friend, when it was his turn, would listen to Mahler and go through every conceivable emotion, ending each piece perspiring and fulfilled.

My second turn I had my first gas bummer. I realized when my friend left the room that if I wanted to, I could probably gas myself to death by refusing to inhale any oxygen and clamping my teeth on the hose. When I decided not to die, I was immediately filled with negative feelings which soon applied themselves to my usual doubts and fears such as sex, goals, etc. But the gas bummer was unlike any other I had experienced. Surprisingly it was encouraging because I felt that I couldn't experience anything worse and yet it wasn't really so bad. And since the effects of the gas were gone within a couple of minutes, I realized that any residual bad feelings were part of the drugless me and presumably could be easily controlled. I had learned a lot about myself and how my mind works.

While taking gas a couple of weeks later, I realized that I was totally dependent on whoever I was with to give me more gas or to stop. To turn the valve on or off. And this feeling of dependence, which I previously would have rejected for ego reasons, was a perfectly acceptable condition. This led to a series of revelations about organized religion and dependence on God and faith. For the first time, I understood the security which one could gain from what I usually thought of as "corrupted Christianity." I was becoming so aware of the equality of all things that it scared me a bit.

Several weeks later I took gas alone for 25 minutes. It was wonderful. Unspeakable and undescribable truths became apparent. At one point I became aware that I had to grab something. There was a noise which had to be stopped. I was sideways. It was the gas that was making the noise and the valve which had to be turned off. I had emerged from the unconscious to the conscious. I realized that gas, in fact, is the merging of those two states. I had always thought in terms of conscious being the opposite of unconscious, but now I learned that they are parts of a continuum. The denial of a major dualism. I became nauseous

Fear of Death. But it went away when I ate some food.

All my revelations came down to the non-rational statement, "All is one."

In the breakdown of dualisms, in the union of opposites, I found much peace and natural happiness. As a child it often took me hours to fall asleep at night. I was afraid of not being conscious. And now I had learned that consciousness and unconsciousness were not to be separated into exclusive categories. I became fascinated by the area on the continuum when the two states are most equally blended. It is very much like the hypnogogic state, the kind of consciousness which occurs just before you fall asleep.

Such a beautiful 25 minutes being alone with nitrous oxide. I created a companion. I burst into exhuberant chanting, I saw through all the illusion and studied a prolonged hypnogogic state. Going up I felt wonderful, coming down I observed my thoughts. It was not threatening to be alone, it was exciting.

My next few gas therapy sessions stressed the basic unity, the "all is one" theme. In other words, 3 = 1. I decided that exhilarating gas was a more appropriate name than laughing gas because laughing is a superficial description of the experience. It only describes what happens externally. I pondered the possibility that man suffers from nitrous oxide deficiency in his "normal" state. Chemical philosophy is a branch of metaphysical research. I realized that the body is nothing more than a mass of chemical reactions and that enlightenment is the realization that death is just a shifting around of molecules.

At one gas celebration, each person took a turn taking it standing up until he lost consciousness with the security that the rest of the group would keep him from injuring himself. One fellow, an Ethiopian, perfected a method of passing out without falling over or even closing his eyes. The evening culminated with nine of us linking arms in a circle. Two people at a time would inhale gas from the hoses connected to the tanks until they passed out. The conscious supported the unconscious and the circle maintained itself for several minutes.

For our next gas celebration, during the winter holiday season, we decided that something had to be done to eliminate the greediness that occurs at large gatherings and the anxiousness which comes about while waiting for the hose to pass around the circle and back to your turn. We bought some balloons, filled them from the tank and passed them around. Not only did this make it possible for any number of people to experience the high simultaneously, but it conserved the gas and eliminated the danger of someone losing consciousness and continuing to receive nitrous oxide into their body from the steady source of the tank. Although this danger was a fairly remote one, we found the balloons to be a reassuring change in our procedure.

I took a balloon alone late at night and tried to write down what I experienced. "It means you think you've done it wrong. You hear the pen write and sounds post-vibrate seemingly endlessly. A million crickets chirping when you are able to hear them. Crickets really raindrops and my equilibrium rotates counter-clockwise. It, the point when rapid sounds seem only one vibration.

STILLS FROM THE FILM *GAS.*

5

You have to defeat the dilemma 'To life or to die'. The living of life negates the necessity to write about it."

It was at about this time that some friends and I became sufficiently curious about nitrous oxide to do some library research on the subject. We were pleased to find that previous users of laughing gas as an exhilarant were, like ourselves, active supporters of revolution against oppressive rule. This in no way surprised us because nitrous oxide has a way of lifting one above everything and seeing things with a cosmic objectivity. Up there, one sees the Ideal and Perfection and when you come back down to "normal consciousness" it is vividly clear who and what is fighting this natural Ideal.

Were it not for the transitory nature of the nitrous oxide experience, this cosmic objectivity might be quite a shock to a normally neurotic person because when one is experiencing the oneness of the universe and then follows this with an image of oneself in daily life, there is usually a large performance gap. But with a bit of self-confidence and determination this view of The Way It Really Is is an invaluable aid toward making one's daily life more honest.

After a second session of writing down my experiences while taking nitrous oxide, I concluded that writing restricted me from reaching the mystical stages because in these stages words become irrelevant. I did however get down on paper some personal revelations.

"When I was taking IQ tests I always scored in the 99th percentile. I scored highest in someone else's game and then realized the falsity of the game."

"For the individual, evolution is learning pertinent information from dead persons."

"Fragmented thought is considered schizophrenic or poetry."

"Forgiveness is the fragrance of a crushed flower." (This was said to me by a middle-aged schizophrenic.)

"Art is the catalyst for communication between conscious and unconscious."

"There is a great difference between longevity and immortality."

As a rule I have found large gas parties to be less enjoyable and less satisfying than taking gas alone or in a small group, but that is the way I feel about large gatherings in general. However, I have had some remarkably positive experiences at gas celebrations of twelve to twenty-five people because communal consciousness can develop and everyone becomes equally your closest friend. The group functions as a single, living organism. Rather than being aware of it being my turn to fill up balloons, I am aware of being an organ which naturally performs its function in keeping the organism alive.

There have been times when I have found myself in a mass of bodies, holding or stroking another body or bodies and being held or stroked by others. I have had no idea which people belonged to which bodies and not only did I not mind this, but I was relieved by it because it banished ego worries and personal relationship conflicts.

6

THE HISTORY OF NITROUS OXIDE

DAVID WALLECHINSKY

Laughing gas was discovered in 1772 by Joseph Priestley, a dissenting minister in Bristol, England. This was a time when men of knowledge sought a well-rounded education rather than a specialized one. Consequently, medical and scientific discoveries were being made by poets and philosophers instead of specialists and experts. Priestley was a gentleman of the first kind and he published studies on electricity, colors, history and education, as well as philosophy and theology.

During a series of experiments in which he also discovered oxygen, Priestley, while trying to determine if dry carbon dioxide would dissolve iron, prepared a mixed gas which he called "Dephlogisticated Nitrous Air." He ran several experiments with the gas, which was later renamed nitrous oxide, but he never inhaled it.

Several years later, in 1791, Priestley's revolutionary views led a mob to burn down his house. His parishioners turned against him, and he settled elsewhere and attempted to build a new laboratory. But when the French Revolution overthrew the aristocracy, the new French Republic honored Priestley as a free citizen and offered him asylum. This did his situation in England no good and he fled to post-revolutionary America where he lived on a farm in Pennsylvania until his death in 1804.

The conflict between radical experimenters on one side and conservative mobs and governments on the other has continued throughout the history of Laughing Gas, and an understanding of the political situation during this early period is important.

England in the late eighteenth century was ruled by a corrupt squirearchy that lived in fear of the French Revolution crossing the Channel. The King was mad and the Prince was a renowned drunk, but the aristocracy put all of its support behind the monarchy rather than risk sharing power with the lower classes. On the other hand, the literary and intellectual population, centered in the port city of Bristol, was open to any replacement of the existent form of government, which flogged, branded and dunked law-breakers.

The second city of England, Bristol was losing much of its trade and commerce to newer ports and newer cities with new industries. However, while London grew in population, Bristol grew in culture, attracting many brilliant minds from England's rural, Western counties.

Bristol was also blessed with hot springs and by the 1790's, the Clifton end of the city had become an expensive spa, drawing the wealthiest and sickest citizens of the country. They came to the Clifton waters as a last resort in their fights against consumption, cancer, palsy and other terminal illnesses.

The presence of a large number of dying, rich aristocrats in turn attracted healers of all sorts: fashionable doctors, exploiters, serious students and experimental physicians.

Thus was Bristol, and specifically the Clifton area, the perfect place for Dr. Thomas Beddoes, poet and father of preventive medicine, to open his Pneumatic Institution, a small experimental hospital and laboratory specializing in treatment by means of gases, primarily oxygen.

Beddoes was born in the village of Shifnal, Shropshire on 13 April, 1760. His father died young and his grandfather, realizing that young Thomas, who could read at the age of five, had scholarly potential, sent him away to a preparatory school at an early age.

When Grandfather Thomas was thrown from a horse, sustaining injuries which developed into general surgical emphysema, Grandson Thomas, though only nine years old, showed great interest in the illness and its treatment and became close friends with the attending surgeon, Mr. Yonge, spending much time with him until the grandfather died a few days later. This was the beginning of Thomas Beddoes' interest in medicine.

After receiving his Bachelor of Arts degree in 1781, Beddoes studied medicine in London and then at Edinburgh. At Edinburgh he was quite popular among the students and in 1785, when a dispute broke out between the Royal Infirmary and the students, Beddoes was chosen to be leader of the protest.

Two years later he was appointed Lecturer in Chemistry at Oxford and he became renowned for his unusual experiments. In one of these, after formulating a theory that the pigmentation of Negroes was due to lack of oxygen in the skin from continued exposure to sunlight, he induced a Negro to dip his fingers in chlorine with the result that the fingers turned white. The experiment was cut short when some sores on the black man's fingers became intolerably irritated.

JOSEPH PRIESTLY (1733-1804). Priestley discovered laughing gas in 1772, during a series of experiments in which he also discovered oxygen. Several years later, Priestley's revolutionary views led a mob to burn down his house. When the french Revolution overthrew the aristocracy, Priestley was offered asylum in France, whereupon he fled England to post-revolutionary America.

It was during his stay at Oxford that Thomas Beddoes made the acquaintance of physician and natural scientist Erasmus Darwin, grandfather of Charles Darwin.

In 1792 Darwin wrote a scientific poem on the *Economy of Vegetation and the Loves of the Plants* which included verses on diverse subjects, including the application of the steam engine to the purposes of coining.

> *With iron lips his rapid rollers seize*
> *The lengthening bars, in thin espansion squeeze;*
> *Descending screws with ponderous fly-wheels wound*
> *The tawny plates, the new medallions round;*

The poem was considered an inimitable masterpiece. This inspired Beddoes to write some lines in the same style and successfully pass them off as Darwin's. Having gained great pleasure from the stunt, he expanded the lines into a 562-line poem entitled *Alexander's Expedition down the Hydaspes and the Indus to the Indian Ocean.* This poem was a complete parody of Darwin's *Economy of Vegetation* including the addition of extensive essays in the form of footnotes, which were far longer than the poem itself.

The alleged purpose of the poem and its footnotes and essays was to "diffuse more widely a knowledge of old and new Hindoo literature" and describe the customs, religion, commercial products, climate and scenery of India. Beddoes, however, had never actually been to India and a deeper purpose to the poem was in fact to be found. Hidden in the footnotes and essays are exposures and denunciations of England's imperialistic treatment of the Hindoos and a plea for an end to English domination of India.

Later in the year, news came to England that the Revolution had taken power in France and that supporters of the monarchy were being massacred. The Reign of Terror horrified Beddoes, but, unlike most of his countrymen, he continued to support the French Republic and openly criticized the English government for declaring war on France. These anti-imperialist, anti-war views were too much for the conservative university at Oxford and Beddoes was forced to leave before the year was out.

After gathering his resources, he traveled to Bristol with the intention of opening a laboratory to test new gases on patients. At first the local residents were hostile to Beddoes and his gases, fearing the laboratory as a threat to life and property, but by May 1793 he had started experimenting with oxygen, using himself as guinea pig.

Beddoes continued to speak out for socialism and better treatment of the poor, complaining that "the groans of the sick form no part of the budget, and Ministers cannot (or perceive not that they can) secure themselves in office by efforts to ease the pangs by which those groans are excited..." In 1795 the

THOMAS BEDDOES.In 1799, Beddoes opened the Pneumatic Institution in Bristol, England to study the therapeutic uses of gases. He was a chemist, a poet, a socialist pamphleteer, a campus protest leader, and a physician. His strong stands against economic imperialism and foreign wars were considered subversive by the conservative administration at Oxford, and Beddoes, although extremely popular with the students, was forced to give up his lectureship in chemistry. Dr. Beddoes reports his observations on the effects of nitrous oxide in Davy's *Researches*: ".... there seemed to be quick and strong alterations in the degree of illumination of all surrounding objects; and I felt as if composed of finely vibrating strings ... immediately afterwards I have often caught myself walking in hurried step and busy in soliloquy. ...." It was Beddoes who hired Humphry Davy as his assistant and gave him equipment and encouragement to pursue his experiments with nitrous oxide.

11

English government, under the leadership of William Pitt, presented the "Gagging Bills," which were intended to prohibit the publication of pamphlets and the holding of free political meetings.

Intellectuals and democrats were enraged and Beddoes fired off two new pamphlets condemning Pitt and the Gagging Bills. These writings formed the basis for public meetings of protest which infuriated the conservative population of Bristol (the number of sick aristocrats was growing). A third pamphlet, urging peace with revolutionary France, insured a grossly biased reception for any news or discoveries which might come out of Beddoes' laboratory.

In addition to his political and social writings, Beddoes continued to publish works on chemistry and medicine. As an appendix to one of these latter publications, he printed an extraordinary essay on nitrous oxide by Samuel Latham Mitchell, a professor in the College of New York, titled: *Remarks on the Gaseous Oxyd of Azote or of Nitrogene, and on the effects it produces, when generated in the stomach, inhaled into the lungs, and applied to the skin. Being an attempt to ascertain the true nature of Contagion, and to explain thereupon the phenomenon of Fever.*

Although Mitchell ran no experiments, he concluded that nitrous oxide was formed by decomposition of digesting meat and fish, that it caused widespread fever and that it was in fact the cause of plague.

By the spring of 1799 Beddoes had raised enough money to open his Pneumatic Institution. To aid him, he chose a twenty-year old friend of a friend named Humphry Davy, a self-educated student of medicine from the rural counties. Davy was born on December 17, 1778, at Penzance, a coinage town of 3000 population, and his childhood was heavily influenced by John Tonkin, an elderly local surgeon who had adopted Humphry Davy's mother. Tonkin was an eccentric who fought modern changes and dressed until his death in the cocked hat, large powdered wig, ruffles and upright collar of the early eighteenth century.

As a teenager, Humphry was apprenticed to a local apothecary and he began his study of chemistry by reading whatever books were available. This included the Beddoes work which contained Mitchell's theory of nitrous oxide. A short period of experimentation quickly disproved the theory and Davy communicated his findings to Beddoes, who eagerly encouraged the young man to join him in Bristol.

Beddoes hired several other assistants, including Peter Mark Roget, who later distinguished himself by developing the theory of persistence of vision which led to motion pictures, and by compiling his famed Thesaurus. But it was Davy who was chosen to be superintendent of the institution. Fortunately his duties were not excessive and he was able to spend most of his time in the laboratory where he immediately began experimenting with nitrous oxide, among other things. From December 1799 to July 1800, Davy manufactured and tested various gases and wrote a six hundred page book describing what he

PETER MARK ROGET, author of the *Thesaurus,* wrote a description of the laughing gas experience which demonstrated both his keen powers of observation and his precise command of the English language:

"The effect of the inspirations of the nitrous oxide was that of making me vertiginous, and producing a tingling sensation in my hands and feet: as these feelings increased, I seemed to lose the sense of my own weight, and imagined I was sinking into the ground. I then felt a drowsiness gradually steal upon me, and a disinclination to motion; even the actions of inspiring and expiring were not performed without effort: and it also required some attention of mind to keep my nostrils closed with my fingers. I was gradually roused from this torpor by a kind of delirium, which came on so rapidly that the air-bag dropped from my hands. This sensation increased for about a minute after I had ceased to breathe, to a much greater degree than before, and I suddenly lost sight of all the objects around me, they being apparently obscured by clouds, in which were many luminous points, similar to what is often experienced on rising suddenly and stretching out the arms, after sitting long in one position.

"I felt myself totally incapable of speaking, and for some time lost all consciousness of where I was, or who was near me. My whole frame felt as if violently agitated: I thought I panted violently: my heart seemed to palpitate, and every artery to throb with violence; I felt a singing in my ears; all the vital motions seemed to be irresistibly hurried on, as if their equilibrium had been destroyed, and every thing was running headlong into confusion. My ideas succeeded one another with extreme rapidity, thoughts rushed like a torrent through my mind, as if their velocity had been suddenly accelerated by the bursting of a barrier which had before retained them in their natural and equable course. This state of extreme hurry, agitation, and tumult, was but transient. Every unnatural sensation gradually subsided; and in about a quarter of an hour after I had ceased to breathe the gas, I was nearly in the same state in which I had been at the commencement of the experiment.

"I cannot remember that I experienced the least pleasure from any of these sensations. I can, however, easily conceive, that by frequent repetition I might reconcile myself to them, and possibly even receive pleasure from the same sensations which were then unpleasant.

"I am sensible that the account I have been able to give of my feelings is very imperfect. For however calculated their violence and novelty were to leave a lasting impression on the memory, these circumstances were for that very reason unfavourable to accuracy of comparison with sensations already familiar.

"The nature of the sensations themselves which bore greater resemblance to a half delirious dream than to any distinct state of mind capable of being accurately remembered, contributes very much to increase the difficulty. And as it is above two months since I made the experiment, many of the minuter circumstances have probably escaped me."

learned. This was **Researches Chemical and Philosophical, chiefly concerning Nitrous Oxide and its Respiration**, part of which has been reprinted as Chapter 7.

Davy, like Beddoes, believed in self-experimentation, which, in the case of nitrous oxide, proved highly pleasurable, though extremely difficult to relate in scientific terms. Indeed, this important period in laughing gas history is best communicated through the words of Davy himself. The day following his first experience with nitrous oxide exhilaration, Davy wrote: "The next morning the recollections of the effects of the gas were very indistinct, and had not remarks written immediately after the experiment recalled them to mind, I should have even doubted of their reality. I was willing to attribute some of the strong emotion to the enthusiasm, which I supposed must have been necessarily connected with the perception of agreeable feelings, when I was prepared to experience painful sensations. Two experiments, however, made in the course of this day, with scepticism, convinced me that the effects were solely owing to the specific operation of the gas.

"Generally when I breathed from six to seven quarts, muscular motions were produced to a certain extent; sometimes I manifested my pleasure by stamping or laughing only, at other times by dancing round the room and vociferating.

"Between May and July, I habitually breathed the gas, occasionally three or four times a day for a week together...the effects appeared undiminished by habit, and were hardly ever exactly similar. Sometimes I had the feeling of intense intoxication, attended with but little pleasure; at other times, sublime emotions connected with vivid ideas.

"At the end of July, I left off my habitual course of respiration, but I continued to breathe the gas, either for the sake of enjoyment, or with the view of ascertaining its operation under particular circumstances.

"In August, I made many experiments with a view toward ascertaining whether any analogy existed between the sensible effects of the different gases which are sooner or later fatal to life when respired, and those of nitrous oxide. . .

"During a fit of enthusiasm produced by the respiration of nitrous oxide, I resolved to endeavour to breathe nitrous gas [an entirely different substance, perhaps nitric oxide. . .]. I transferred my mouth from the mouthpiece of the bag to that of the air-holder, and turning the stop-cock, attempted to inspire the nitrous gas. After moving my lips from the mouthpiece, when I opened them to inspire common air, aeriform nitrous acid was instantly in my mouth, which burnt the tongue and palate, injured the teeth, and produced an inflammation of the mucous membranes which lasted some hours. . . I never design again to attempt so rash an experiment.

"To ascertain with certainty, whether the most extensive action of nitrous

14

oxide is compatible with life, was capable of producing debility, I resolved to breathe the gas for such a time and in such quantities, as to produce excitement equal in duration and superior in intensity to that occasioned by high intoxication from opium or alcohol. To habituate myself to the excitement, and to carry it on gradually, on December 26th I was enclosed in an air-tight breathing box, of the capacity of about 9 cubic feet, in the presence of Dr. Kinglake. . . . My emotions were enthusiastic and sublime. . . ."

Davy goes on: "At night I found myself unusually cheerful and active... In bed I enjoyed profound repose. When I awoke in the morning, it was with consciousness of pleasurable existence, and this consciousness more or less continued through the day.

"I have often felt very great pleasure when breathing it alone, in darkness and silence, occupied only by ideal existence.

"On May 5th, at night, after walking for an hour amidst the scenery of the Avon, at this period rendered exquisitely beautiful by bright moonshine, my mind being in a state of agreeable feeling, I respired six quarts of newly prepared nitrous oxide. The thrilling was very rapidly produced. The objects around me were perfectly distinct, and the light of the candle not as usual dazzling. The pleasurable sensation was at first local, and perceived in the lips and about the cheeks. It gradually, however, diffused itself over the whole body, and in the middle of the experiment was for a moment so intense and pure as to absorb existence. At this moment, and not before, I lost consciousness; it was, however, quickly restored, and I endeavoured to make a by-stander acquainted with the pleasure I experienced by laughing and stamping.

"I have sometimes experienced from nitrous oxide, sensations similar to no others, and they have consequently been indescribable. This has been likewise often the case with other persons. Of two paralytic patients who were asked what they felt after breathing nitrous oxide, the first answered, 'I do not know how, but very queer.' The second said, 'I felt like the sound of a harp.'

It should be noted that Beddoes' circle of friends, and thus Davy's too, was quite a distinguished one, including the poets S. T. Coleridge and Robert Southey, the inventor James Watt, Joseph Priestley's son, and numerous other poets and artists and scientists. So, when Davy's experiments reached the point of human inhalation, he had a highly creative group of volunteers to experiment on. Their reactions and impressions of the gas are also included by Davy in his book.

Word of Davy's experiments spread quickly and soon patients were flocking to the Pneumatic Institution to be treated with the gas of paradise. The conservative elements of the Bristol population were appalled by the carnival atmosphere that developed within the institution. Their suspicions about the radical Beddoes and his effect on the neighborhood were confirmed. A young woman was seen running out of the institution, pursued by male

THE PNEUMATIC INSTITUTION IN 1948   This was the site of the first experiments with nitrous oxide as laughing gas. When Beddoes announced his plans to use the buildings for medical experimentation, the local residents, fearing a degeneration of the neighborhood, were hostile to him. This attitude was not cooled by the appearance of a Negro beggar in front of the Institution who told passers-by that he had been decoyed inside and made the subject of cruel and unheard of experiments. The neighbors were particularly upset one day when a young lady dashed out of the Pneumatic Institution, ran down the road and leaped over a large dog before being retrieved by her friends. A contemporary wrote, "The Pneumatic Institution at this time, from the laughable and diversified effects produced by this new gas on different individuals, converted the laboratory into the region of hilarity and relaxation." Of the Pneumatic Institution and public reaction to the nitrous oxide experiments, Beddoes wrote, "It could not therefore escape me that the pursuit might, in its own nature, be highly rational, and yet that those who first engaged in it might never strike the right path. It was plain that we might even prepare a happier aera for mankind, and yet earn from the mass of our contemporaries nothing better than the title of enthusiasts."

friends. She was not overcome until she had leapt over a large dog. At this point Davy and his fellows experienced a sharp decrease in female volunteers.

In addition to these troubles, the institution was plagued by the appearance of a black beggar in front of its doors who told passers-by that he had been "decoyed thither" and made, without his knowledge, the subject of a cruel and unheard-of experiment. Beddoes had repeated his experiment of placing a black's arm in chlorine to see if it turned white. This man had scratches on his arm which became so painful that he pulled out of the experiment.

In March of 1801, on the basis of his published work on nitrous oxide, Davy was appointed lecturer in chemistry at the Royal Institution of Great Britain in London, a branch of the Society for Bettering the Condition of the Poor. He gave one or two lectures on the gas and then turned to other subjects, never to study laughing gas again. Without him, the Pneumatic Institution deteriorated quickly and closed. Beddoes continued his research elsewhere, but ne died a largely rejected man.

Davy went on to further successes, discovering potassium and inventing the safety lantern still used by miners. He refused to patent the lantern because he had vowed years earlier never to make a profit from science. He was, however, made *Sir* Humphrey Davy and eventually he was awarded a baronetcy.

Laughing gas was sent into seclusion by conservative repression and its use was limited to medical students in England and the United States.

In the 1840's laughing gas reappeared as a form of public entertainment in America. "Itinerant chemists," some of them sideshow performers, some of them sincere teachers, toured the country giving lectures on laughing gas and electricity and demonstrating the effects of both on volunteers from the audience. At one of these exhibitions, given by Gardner Quincy Colton in Hartford, Connecticut, there was in the audience a young dentist named Horace Wells. One of the volunteers who stepped onto the stage to inhale the gas, a carpenter named Cooley, smashed his shin against a settee while dancing about in joy. Wells was immediately struck by the fact that Cooley seemed to exhibit no signs of pain and that it was not until the effects of the gas wore off that he became aware of his injury.

Wells approached Colton on the subject and arranged to have a wisdom tooth extracted while Colton administered gas. The operation was a success and Wells, upon regaining consciousness, is said to have exclaimed, "A new era in tooth-pulling!" He was urged by friends to patent his discovery, but refused, declaring, "No! Let it be as free as the air we breathe!"

Wells gave a demonstration of nitrous oxide anesthesia at Harvard Medical College, but the patient cried out and Wells' discovery was dismissed in Boston despite the admission by the patient that he had not actually experienced any pain. Wells returned to Hartford and continued his use of the gas for tooth extractions. An article in the June 18, 1845 edition of the Boston Medical and Surgical Journal reported, "The nitrous oxyd gas has been used in quite a

DR. GARDNER Q. COLTON. In the 1840's Colton toured the East
Coast conducting lectures and demonstrations on N_2O. Twenty years
later, Colton and a partner opened the first clinic devoted to dental
extraction with nitrous oxide.

number of cases by dentists, during the extraction of teeth, and has been found by its excitement, perfectly to destroy pain; the patients appear very merry during the operation, and no unpleasant effects follow."

Most of the remaining three and a half years of Horace Wells' life were spent defending his discovery of nitrous oxide as a pain-killer against the claims of his former student and partner, William Morton. In January of 1848 Wells was visited by a friend whose suit of clothing had been ruined by a New York prostitute who had thrown some acid on him. The friend sought revenge and convinced Wells to give him some acid and accompany him to Broadway, where the young man found the lady in question and sprinkled acid on her shawl. The man wanted to expand the acid-throwing and drive the street-walkers out of the neighborhood, but Wells refused to cooperate any further.

On January 21 Wells, while under the influence of chloroform and general melancholia, was arrested for throwing acid at local streetwalkers. He was consumed with guilt over the act, and two days later, in his cell, he committed suicide by slashing his left thigh and severing the femoral artery after preparing himself for the deed by inhaling a vial of chloroform.

Colton, meanwhile, worked at a variety of jobs around the country before returning to laughing gas exhibitions in 1863. In his lectures he always told the story of Wells and the painless extraction, and one day a woman with a bad toothache asked if she might be given laughing gas while having her tooth pulled. The operation was a success and by 1868 Colton and a partner had performed 75,000 extractions using nitrous oxide. Finally the gas caught on as a pain-killer and its use spread until today it is the most commonly used general anesthetic in surgery.

As its use as a pain-killer spread, its use as an exhilarant was driven underground, fear of pleasure being one of the major cultural traits of the past century.

However, laughing gas has always continued to be used by certain groups, notably medical students, hospital orderlies, and philosophical experimenters.

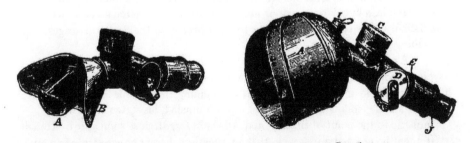

FIG. 1.   FIG. 2.

Codman & Shurtleff's Inhalers for Nitrous Oxide.

FIG. 1.—Inhaler for Nitrous Oxide Gas: A, hard-rubber mouth-piece; B, metallic hood.
FIG. 2.—A, metallic hood; B, flexible rubber hood, projecting from within the metallic face-piece; C, exhaling-valve; D. two-way stop-cock; I. packing, through which a silk cord passes; E, sliding-joint, where J is detached to connect the ether-reservoir; J contains the inhaling-valve.

19

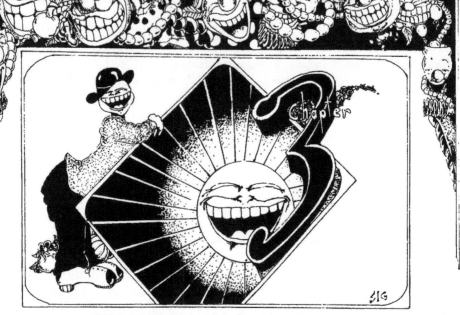

THE EFFECTS OF NITROUS OXIDE
by William Lopez

Let us consider Clement's account of the effects of N_2O along with the onset of slight oxygen deprivation: "A sense of warmth, well-being, or exhilaration occurs. The tongue feels thickened and the speech is guttural. The touch and pressure senses are present, but sounds become distant and terminal nerve pain is abolished. Entrance into the excitement stage is indicated by a tendency to laugh, shout, sing, or to exhibit violent muscular movements. Loss of memory occurs early. Muscular power is lost gradually . . . the senses are lost one by one, hearing usually the last to go."

Directly upon inspiration of N_2O, one experiences a distancing from the immediate environment — the room and its objects no longer demand specification or relevance, even though they continue to register visually. Sound patterns fragment and disintegrate, random noises are amplified and distorted. This throbbing, phaser-like distortion is one of the truly distinguishing characteristics of nitrous oxide. At certain times during an N_2O voyage, hearing is the only functioning sense. Occasionally the nature of the more profound psychical reaction to the N_2O will be determined by a single imposing sound; for example, a knock on the door might conjure a hallucinated scenario with sufficient intensity to cause the user to react overtly to the fantastic images resulting from the sound.

As one breathes more of the gas, a number of reactions are common. The voice becomes deeper and thicker. The N_2O user feels a desire to blurt out the most accessible of the revelations that are spinning through his brain. If he does speak, and depending on the amount of N_2O inhaled, his statement is often emphatic to the point of finality, and is usually forgotten as soon as it is uttered. (It might be pointed out as well, that a perfectly coherent conversation can take place under the influence.) The inhaler feels increasing generalized excitement and enthusiasm, complemented by a decreasing concern for extra-corporal and non-sensual matters. Auditory interference by now has become a cacophony of scrambled external sounds and equally convincing hallucinated entries.

Visual hallucinations can occur with the first few lungfuls of gas, although they are perhaps most potent at the point when the user regains "consciousness" after having passed out for a few seconds (the zenith of the gas experience). Mild nitrous oxide hallucinations are somewhat similar to intense LSD, DMT, THC, and marijuana hallucinations — richly colored geometric phantasms, police sirens, a wall melts, a table moves, a person appears in the corner of an eye. Medium intensity N_2O visions may include the coordinated jerking and flashing of all that one sees, i.e., a fully appointed room may appear to jump suddenly toward the user, then jump away again, like a flickering old movie projected at frantically shifting angles and distances from the viewer. The user may feel close to blacking out, not an unpleasant experience if one is accepting of it. Medium intensity N_2O hallucinations can be quite similar to dreams — the user may find himself in a totally fabricated environment, interacting with a cast of seemingly real people.

In regard to nitrous oxide and dreams, I refer to Ouspensky's categorization of dreams. He divides them into three types:

1) the chaos or nonsense dream — unrelated images or bits of images that are quite probably more related to immediate or environmental conditions than to profound subconscious energy;

2) the dramatic or story dream — structure, characters, and often a complete story; perhaps this is the artist in us screaming in the night;

3) the revelation dream — one sees God or receives a grand insight into the mystery of existence; these appear to be infrequent.

The visions experienced during intense levels of nitrous oxide exhilaration seem to be a meld of the chaotic dream and the revelation dream, those two categories that would seem to be the most remote from classical symbolic interpretation. In other words, gas is not really like conventional dramatic dreams; visions are fragmented and often have the aura of revelation. Frederik Van Eeden's definition of a *lucid dream* provides a focus for a description of the non-mystical nitrous oxide visions. (**Proc. Soc. Psych. Res.**, 1913). "In these lucid dreams the reintegration of the psychic functions is so complete that the sleeper remembers day-life and his own condition, reaches a state of perfect awareness and is able to direct his attention, and to attempt different acts of free volition." Under the influence of N_2O, at a particularly intense, yet pre-mystical stage of exhilaration, the user does retain a secure image of his own real-life, his own normal existence; he/she retains the power to direct actions and thoughts; yet he/she is still imbedded in a situation, a vision, a dream. One is often aware of sitting in a room full of people, and of inspiring N_2O, yet one cannot deny the definite half-dream or hallucinatory milieu produced by the gas. Van Eeden claimed that all his lucid dreams were accompanied by the feeling of flight. Often, during the nitrous oxide exhilaration, one experiences sensations of floating, whirling, or flying. The setting during these sensations is frequently an infinite vacuum or void, astral blue or neutral gray. Usually, unless some degree of hearing is retained, the void through which one floats is conspicuously silent. In my experience with these flying sensations, the void itself was empty of all objects besides my person, and was finite — is seemed to be some ten to thirty feet in diameter and was itself spinning slowly through a similar, much larger vacuum. There was no fear of falling involved.

More often than a floating sensation, I have experienced a rushing feeling — I am being propelled, upright, through unidentifiable time and space at an extremely high rate of speed, only to arrive back at my nitrous oxide party. A frivolous metaphor for this abrupt re-entry into normal waking consciousness is the image and sound of the Roadrunner shooting up to an arbitrary spot in the road and stopping dead to the sound of a snapped board. This is the wondrous sensation that N_2O provides of having effortlessly traversed great distances in less than a moment.

I have found that gas-induced hallucinations can involve literally anything. In this respect I'd like to mention Aldous Huxley's discussion of the philosopher C.D. Broad's interpretation of Bergson's theory that the brain and nervous system perform an essentially "eliminative" function. Broad says that everyone is capable of sensing all occurrences in the universe and of remembering everything that has ever happened to him. The nervous system protects us from being overamped and blown out by such a gigantic quantity of information, and eliminates enough of it to permit us to function practically on a day-to-day level. "According to such a theory," says Huxley, "each one of us is potentially Mind at Large." However, man creates and embellishes languages, "those symbol-systems and implicit philosophies", to "formulate and express the contents of his reduced awareness." (Huxley). Most consciousness is utilitarian and language-oriented, and actively denies the irrational and the mystical. However, temporary passes to the realms of Mind at Large can be obtained by some persons spontaneously, through spiritual exercises, through hypnosis, or through psychedelic drugs. Nitrous oxide, particularly, seems to induce a high frequency of such aberrant conditions — quickly, without great effort, and above all, safely if used prudently. The "without great effort" clause may seem to invalidate the experience in the eyes of the Calvinist Western World. How can such a facile experience be truly profound? My advice is to try it.

Gas is, in no sense, "bottled or pre-digested wisdom," to borrow Alan Watts' phrase. Gas is not The Way, nor will it get rid of the nubs, put you in the driver's seat, or keep you dry for twenty-four hours. Gas, aside from inducing deep personal revelations, allows "the contents of consciousness to happen without interference." (Watts). Gas precipitates spontaneous movement that is normally stifled by considerations of social propriety. Gas puts one in brief touch with the energy of the universe, and "enables the individual to be so peculiarly open and sensitive to organic reality that the ego begins to be seen for the transparent abstraction that it is." (Watts).

It seems to me narrow, impractical, dangerous, and ultimately unreal to live perpetually in the sane world of guilt, fear, accomplishment, etiquette, language, ego, rationality, and utility, and to deny the Mysterium Tremendum, the Mind at Large, the realms of atom-dreams and demon-engines, the "multi-dimensional superconsciousness" that has been the subject of some of the most assiduous and intense investigations of human history.

Of course, when the gas leaves your body you are returned to "everyday reality," and must again function as a member of society. Our simple contention is not that the nitrous oxide experience is superior to normal consciousness, but that it is *different* and *positive*, enriching one's awareness of Self and Other, and better equipping one to be Real, to proceed toward what one *wants* rather than where one is *supposed* to be going.

A word about the nitrous oxide bummer. During a bad gas trip, which seems inevitable sooner or later, the visions tend toward the more dramatic — more toward emotional involvement and identification with oneself as portrayed in the dream. Chaos and revelation coalesce, and are somehow structured through characters and events into actual ego confrontations. It is not my contention that the bad trip results from the structuring of the vision, but rather that the many N_2O bad trips are simply ego-dramas, where essence and persona plunge from consciousness to unconsciousness and back too fast for ego control; the drama is chaotic. It is compressed and intense, and it is enhanced by the revelationary quality of nitrous oxide.

Gas bummers are ultimately dissimilar to Van Eeden's "demon dreams" and more like his descriptions of "mocking or symbolic dreams." In Van Eeden's mocking dreams, the sleeper is plagued by discomfitting and distasteful inventions. "Nothing is too low or horrible for such dreams," says Van Eeden. The sleeper is a murderer or an outcast, and is harrassed by doubts. In the demon dream, these symbolic monsters are more visible and accessible, and the dreamer can identify and challenge them, rendering their power less portentous and mythical. Van Eeden remarks about his demon dreams: "I *see* the demons and fight them; the effect is thoroughly pleasing."

Certain N_2O visions in which "demons" or symbolic chimeras appear are quite amusing — I have had indescribable creatures jump directly out of the wall at me with such vividness that my only recourse was to cover my head with both arms, jump away, and become unconscious. These creatures were fascinating, full-fledged visions, in other words, they were so potent that I lost the sense of experiencing an hallucination — I experienced only the demon and my reaction to it. I could not say to myself *at the instant of occurrence* that I was simply seeing an hallucination. So, as Van Eeden observed, there is nothing

AN AMBITIOUS PLAN FOR A NITROUS OXIDE CARRIAGE. (Probably late 1800's.)

to fear from an out-and-out demon, and viewing one is invariably quite an extraordinary delight.

The gas bummer is more like Van Eeden's symbolic or mocking dream it is saturated in turpitude and suffering, but often the causes or solutions to the painful situations are recondite or hopeless, rendering the subject despondent and confounded. However, these bummers are highly instructive to anyone who experiences them, because they illuminate repressed areas of the consciousness.

One of the things nitrous oxide can do in social situations is to break down traditional constrictions and inhibitions surrounding social gatherings. By this I don't mean to imply a high incidence of orgies, but rather a disregard for conventional social-party roles   host-guest, adult-adolescent, seductor-seductee — these become trivial and inconsequential. As opposed to the cocktail party, for instance, I have attended N_2O affairs where perhaps a dozen people lay sprawled in a pile in the middle of the room — silent, smiling, nodding, and leisurely passing big party balloons filled with gas. This seems to me positive in the extreme as it provides direct experience of alternative forms of group behavior. Solo dancing, singing, both in falsetto and in basso, jumping, stamping, throwing up the arms, non-erotic fondling, incoherent verbal outbursts, passing out, and any number of ecstatic "mindless" fiddlings are commonplace at gas parties. In Social situations with gas, we see ourselves and our friends doing the kinds of things that we would normally censure and consider uncool. These activities transcend those occurring from conventional intoxication from alcohol, grass, or downers.

R.E. Shor, in the **Am. J. of Psychotherapy**, 1959, states that the generalized reality-orientation is a "structured complex of recollections, an abstractive superstructure of ideas or superordinate gestalt of interrelationships. From its totality are derived various concepts and functions, some of which are reality-testing, body-image, critical self-awareness; cognition of self, world, other people, time, space, logic, purpose, various inhibitions, conscious fears, and defenses." Shor claims that the idea of *self* has no sensible meaning unless situated within a substantive orientation to reality, and that reality orientation *is*, in a sense, "reality."

In certain states, commonly called trances, this generalized reality-orientation dissolves into "relatively nonfunctional unawareness " (Shor). In the case of a hypnotic trance, one's attention becomes focused on a limited body of preoccupations, and concomitantly, reality-orientation assumes a subordinate position, "so that certain behaviors can function in isolation from the totality of generalized experiences " (Shor). In a profound nitrous oxide trance, however, while reality-orientation is definitely wiped out, it is not replaced by a particular set or range of preoccupations. The user is momentarily set free not only from sensory inputs, but from "reality" altogether. Even cognition of self,

25

conscious fears, and awareness of time and space melt away, allowing the subject to drift in a mist of consciousness that is separated from his/her being — pure consciousness, not adulterated or bounded by ego, the fear of death, or any other arbiter of reality. In this state, one can fleetingly recognize and merge with other non-corporal conscious energy, be it collective or omniscient.

It has often been asserted that the mystical states achieved by those trained persons who deliberately seek them are phenomenologically indistinguishable from the states achieved by untrained experimenters through psycholytic chemicals.

The question is whether or not the nitrous oxide condition is genuinely mystical. We suggest that it is. W.N. Pahnke and W.A. Richards have attempted to establish the characteristics of the "mystical experience." All of these qualities likewise characterize the nitrous oxide experience.

1) UNITY. The dichotomy between subject and object is transcended. The self and the perceived world cease to exist as separate entities. The brain becomes the mind.

2) OBJECTIVITY and REALITY. When one receives a mystical revelation, one knows and feels that it is true, and not that it is a subjective delusion. The subject accepts its ultimate veracity intuitively.

3) TRANSCENDENCE of SPACE and TIME. Temporal and environmental orientations are out the window during the mystical trance. The user may feel that he/she can look into the past or the future, or may not recognize a difference between the two.

4) SENSE of SACREDNESS. Pahnke and Richards describe sacredness as "a nonrational, intuitive, hushed, palpitant response in the presence of inspiring realities. It is that which a person feels to be of special value and capable of being profaned."

5) DEEPLY FELT POSITIVE MOOD. Joy, ecstacy and exhilaration.

6) PARADOXICALITY. The mystical subject will accept logical contradictions as true despite controverting evidence or sensation. Pahnke and Richards: "He may claim to have experienced an empty unity that at the same time contains all reality."

7) ALLEGED INEFFABILITY. Mystical consciousness seems to transcend articulation; subjects claim that language cannot express their experience.

8) TRANSIENCY. Mystical consciousness is generally of a short duration, a few seconds to a few hours.

(Note on 7 and 8: The most profound stage of the anesthetic condition seems to be largely beyond memory; it can only be recalled when it is induced again. We came across someone who swore that he had never had nitrous oxide; we gave him some, and only then did he remember having had the experience some ten years earlier at a dentist's office. As B.P. Blood asserts, the nitrous oxide consciousness "cannot be brought out of that condition into the normal sanity of sense — cannot be formally remembered, but remains informal, forgotten until we return to it.")

9) POSITIVE CHANGES IN ATTITUDE AND/OR BEHAVIOR. Quoting Pahnke and Richards: "Increased personality integration . . . renewed sense of personal worth . . . relaxation of habitual mechanisms of ego defense . . . one's faith in one's own ability for creative achievement tends to be increased . . . increased vocational commitment . . . (one finally knows) the meaning of meeting another person without the subtle masks that separate man from man . . . increased sensitivity to the inner imperative . . . loss of fear of death coupled with an expanded awareness of the significance of historical existence . . . enriched appreciation for the whole of creation . . . "

All of the above characteristics of mystical consciousness, without exception, can result from exploration of the nitrous oxide experience.

For the sake of further describing the nitrous oxide condition, it is possible to claim that the N_2O experience, particularly with regard to its religious or mystical characteristics, is quite similar to the LSD-mescaline experience with two important distinctions. First, the N_2O-induced state is generally shorter — a blinding momentary flash of insight, without an extended period of swelling mystical emotions. Secondly, the N_2O religious experience is intense to the point of rendering the user "unconscious," passed out, or in an unseeing trance. In other words, gas is very much like acid pushed to its extreme and compressed into a few moments. On gas you have little time to prepare for or reflect on the joyful insight; and it is much more difficult to "maintain" under the influence of gas because it so rapidly and completely suspends everyday reality as well as motor functions.

Alan Watts, in an essay on psychedelics and religious experience in **Does It Matter?**, describes his feelings during a chemically induced mystical state in terms that apply directly to the N_2O condition. He claims four characteristics of the mystical experience:

1) "Concentration in the present" — "One's normally compulsive concern for the future decreases, and one becomes aware of the enormous importance and interest of what is happening at the moment . . . one realizes that the whole point of life is to be fully aware of it as it happens . . . " With gas, the usually unsettling drives for accomplishment in the near future disappear. The concept of productivity and its concomitant guilts, fears, and frustrations dissolve in a moment of timeless bliss. One is freed, for an instant, from trepidation about tomorrow, and, by extension, from the dread of death itself. "Undistracted," in Huxley's phrase, "by the memory of past sins, by imagined pleasures, by the bitter aftertaste of old wrongs and humiliations, by all the fears and hates and cravings that ordinarily eclipse the Light." (**Doors of Perception**).

2) "Awareness of Polarity" — this is a variation of the Stace-Pahnke-Richards primary characteristic of unity. Watts calls this feeling "the vivid

27

realization that states, things, and events which we ordinarily call opposite are interdependent, like back and front or the poles of a magnet." Things which are "explicitly different are implicitly one." Under the influence of nitrous oxide gas, one ceases to feel that one's body is arbitrarily separated from one's immediate and cosmological environment. The everyday tendency is to assume that all of one's facilities, energies, impulses, and ego functions are inside, and everything else is outside. On gas, one becomes intensely and incontrovertably aware that internal, blood-rhythm-energy is interdependent with the molecular, atomic swirling of everything that surrounds the body. One feels as if one is a generator and a receiver of the eco-energy, rather than a self-contained unit standing apart from all "external" persons and objects.

3) "Awareness of Relativity" — Says Watts: "I see that I am a link in an infinite hierarchy of processes and beings, ranging from molecules through bacteria and insects to human beings, and, maybe, to angels and gods. . . ." He goes on: "All forms of life and being are simply variations of a single theme, we are all in fact one being doing the same thing in as many ways as possible." Nitrous oxide intoxication produces a state in which the user feels that he/she is a tone or a pulse or a shade of this grand being, this great form, this awesome energy that *is* the Universe.

4) "Awareness of eternal energy," often in the form of intense white light, which seems to be both the current in your nerves and that mysterious e which equals mc squared." Watts claims that "one sees clearly that all existence is a single energy, and that this energy is one's own being." While this seems contradictory to the concept that one is simply a part of a whole, both emotions are different ways of experiencing the same thing, specifically that each person actually *is* the whole, a concept basic to Hinduism and nitrous oxide. Gas allows you to see that you are ultimately all you've got, that you are indeed the Universe itself.

In discussing his experiences with LSD, Dr. Watts has presented a cogent, if unintended and incomplete description of the most intense level of the anesthetic trance. I have quoted fragments of his writing in an attempt to elucidate the proximity of the LSD-induced religious experiences to those facilitated by N_2O. I want to emphasize that the LSD and N_2O experiences are quite similar at their most powerful moments, particularly in terms of cosmological and personal revelation. With regard to tactile, erotic and aesthetic excitement, acid is considerably more amusing and fulfilling, whereas nitrous oxide provides a greater frequency of mystical experiences. This is not to imply that heightened aesthetic pleasure is foreign to the gas trip, particularly in the acoustical realms, but simply that I have found it more enjoyable and profitable to feel something, to study a painting or read under the influence of psychedelics other than N_2O.

In addition to inducing mystical experiences, opening up new regions of consciousness, and contributing to a general lessening of dependence on external learned-reward patterns, nitrous oxide is very merry indeed. It is one 28 of the few *substances* I know of that can generate ecstacy.

THE PHARMACOLOGY OF NITROUS OXIDE AND
RECOMMENDATIONS FOR SAFE INSPIRATIONS

NITROUS OXIDE (N_2O, laughing gas, nitrogen monoxide, nitrous air) is an inorganic, colorless gas made by heating ammonium nitrate crystals to 190 degrees C. until fused, then at 240 degrees C., yielding N_2O of approximately 95% purity.

$$NH_4NO_3 \qquad 240^\circ \text{ C.} \qquad N_2O + 2H_2O$$

Impurities include nitrogen, nitrogen dioxide, nitric oxide, ammonia, and water vapor. Although official U.S. pharmacological standards indicate 97% purity as permissible, contemporary purification processes usually obtain at least 99.5% purity.

Nitrous oxide has a molecular weight of 44.02; a boiling point of (-)88.44°C.; amd a specific gravity of 1.53. Viscosity (absolute at 0 degrees C.) is 135 micropoises, and (relative to water at 20 degrees C.) is 0.014. Nitrous oxide has a critical pressure of 71.7 atm., a critical temperature of 36.5°C., and a vapor pressure [at (-)88.44°C.] of one atm. (at 27.4°C.: 60 atm.) The density of nitrous oxide (liquid at 0 degrees C.) is 0.8 gm/L. The latent heat of evaporation is 98.6 cal/gm. The specific heat (thermal capacity per degree C. at 15 degrees C.) is 0.20 cal/gm. The heat of formation is (-)17 kilo cal/gm. mol. wt.

Nitrous oxide solubility ratios:

oil/gas — 1.4	blood/gas	— 0.468	
oil/water — 3.2	water/gas	— 0.435	
oil/blood — 3.0	tissue/blood—heart	— 1.3	
	brain	— 1.06	
	lungs	— 1.0	

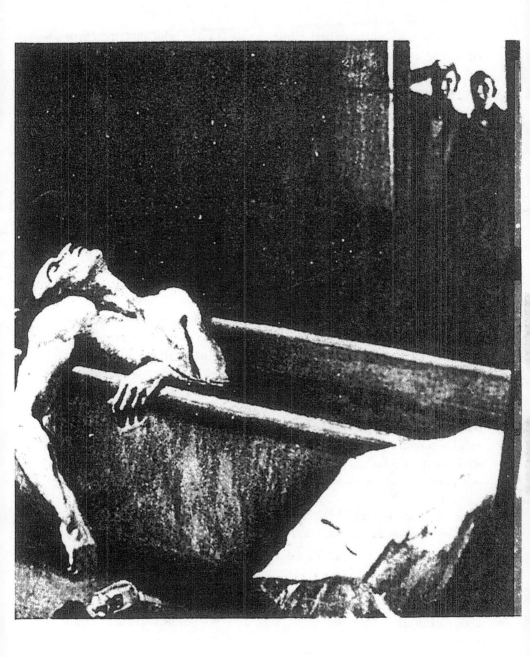

If you follow the precautions in this chapter this won't happen to you. This picture contains an erroneous account of the suicide of Horace Wells. Wells conducted an unsuccessful demonstration of the anesthetic properties of the gas; he was despondent. When he committed suicide three years later it was not in a bathtub as pictured here. In actuality the poor fellow committed the deed while lying on a bed in a prison cell.

In its medical capacities, nitrous oxide is a powerful analgesic (pain killer) and a weak anesthetic, and must be breathed in large quantities to effect general anesthesia. It has a potency of 25% when compared to a drug the potency of diethyl ether.

Nitrous oxide is usually administered with 20-35% oxygen, and can be inhaled for extended periods of time, provided the patient is given enough oxygen. For major surgery, the patient is generally put to sleep before N_2O administration with pentothal or a similar sedative, but unsupplemented N_2O can be used for a variety of operations in which minimal muscular relaxation is required: dental extractions and drainage of abcess, breast biopsy, uterine curettage, vaginal plastic repair, and as an analgesic in obstetrics. Pure nitrous oxide is often administered for brief dental operations.

Induction of and recovery from nitrous oxide are quite rapid; the gas takes effect almost immediately, and fades out of the system in less than a half hour. The actual high lasts one or two minutes.

Nitrous oxide itself is a harmless and innocuous substance. The principal, if not the only danger related to its use is oxygen deprivation (anoxia, hypoxia, asphyxia). Severe decerebration and even death can result from oxygen lack, and although the death percentage throughout twenty decades of medical N_2O use is infinitesimal, a great myth has grown up around the dangers of nitrous oxide. Before dealing with oxygen deprivation, it might be useful to run down just exactly how nitrous oxide affects the system. (An unfortunate gap exists here: no one knows how the anesthetic or the exhilaratingeffects of N_2O are produced in the brain, other than it has to do with the metabolism of the brain cells. This is not obscure or classified information, this simply is not known.)

Sources: John Adriani, M.D., **The Pharmacology of Anesthetic Drugs**
Donald Eastwood, ed., **Nitrous Oxide,** Clinical Anesthesia Series

EFFECTS OF NITROUS OXIDE

BRAIN — N_2O affects all modalities of sensation. Various mentation abilities are affected, such as short-term memory and concentration. Slightly distorted acuity of hearing, sight, and touch occur. Overall electroencephalographic changes are slight.
INTRACRANIAL PRESSURE — No change without anoxia.
TEMPERATURE REGULATING CENTER — Not affected according to Eastwood; slightly depressed during profound anesthesia according to Adriani.
VASOMOTOR CENTER — Not affected without anoxia.
RESPIRATORY CENTER — Not significantly affected without anoxia: slight increase in volume of respiration during administration of unsupplemented N_2O.

COUGH CENTER — Not affected; cough is moderately suppressed.

VOMITING CENTER — Incidence variously reported. Nausea unusual without anoxia.

REFLEXES–VAGUS CENTER — Not affected.

REFLEXES–CAROTID BODY — Not affected.

REFLEXES–CAROTID SINUS — Not affected.

EYES — No affect on size of pupil. Pupils dilated with anoxia, but eyeballs remain active. Intra-ocular tension not affected. Tear secretion mildly depressed.

SALIVARY GLANDS — Insignificantly affected.

CILIA — Activity not decreased without anoxia.

HEART — Rate unaffected. Cardiac output unaffected. Coronary arteries, cardiac muscle, and automatic tissue unchanged. No appreciable electro-cardiographic changes have been demonstrated as a result of nitrous oxide.

BLOOD PRESSURE — Not affected without anoxia.

VENOUS PRESSURE — No elevation of central venous pressure has been demonstrated. Marked elevation if anoxia is present.

LUNGS — N_2O does not irritate pulmonary epithelium. Respiratory movements are not depressed or exaggerated. Bronchial musculature is not affected.

METABOLISM — Not significantly changed.

DIAPHRAGM — Movements not affected.

ADRENAL — Not affected.

STOMACH — Gastric movements unchanged.

INTESTINES — Contractions increase slightly in amplitude and frequency.

LIVER — Functions are not affected unless anoxia is present.

KIDNEY — No significant effects, no significant alterations in volume or composition of urine.

SPLEEN — Not affected.

UTERUS — Rhythmicity, tone or frequency of contractions not inhibited.

GENITALIA — No affects.

SKELETAL MUSCLES — Increased muscle tone, apparently due to altered consciousness, can occur.

SKIN — Slight dilation of skin vessels. The Eastwood text attributes this to "psychic disturbance and altered consciousness."

There is some evidence that a tolerance to N_2O develops after repeated or prolonged administration. Eastwood states: "Clinical observations . . . of rats exposed . . . " revealed that "the animals remained relatively asleep and inactive for the first 12-24 hours, following which they could be more easily aroused and consumed more water and food." (**Nitrous Oxide**, Davis.) Any user of N_2O as an exhilarant can testify that a definite tolerance does in fact develop. After several long sessions, the user may find that as much as 35% more gas will be needed to reach the desired level of consciousness. It must be stressed,

33

however, that no withdrawal symptoms occur and tolerance in no way signifies dependence.

Originally, we planned to include a lengthy section on oxygen deprivation to impress readers and potential critics with our technical knowledge. In the end, however, hypoxemia, anoxia, histotoxic hypoxia, and O_2 apnea are easy to say. Much has been said, all of it relating to the tribulations of professional anesthetists; much undoubtedly will be said, based largely upon existing medical references dealing solely with the problems of anesthesia.

The East Bay Chemical Philosophy Symposium's dozen or so members have consumed some 500,000 quarts of nitrous air throughout 1968, 1969 and 1970. Not one has reported any of the kinds of damage that can result from oxygen deprivation. We are all functioning.

There always lurks the individual negative physical reaction to any potent chemical agent — one's body simply will not tolerate some drug; but this is rare with nitrous oxide, which remains the most common general anesthetic, and such a risk is-assumed when taking any matter into the body. You might ask, "What about long-term use?" B.P. Blood used N_2O throughout his life and continued to write and publish well into his 80's.

It must be remembered, with all due respect, that the physicians who write about the dangers of nitrous oxide do so through exhaustive observation and study of traditional literature, not through personal experimentation. The same authorities who write about the hazards of nitrous oxide draw up tables comparing the nitrous oxide experience to beer and martinis. It should also be noted that the dangers which worry doctors occur because they try to keep patients unconscious for long periods, a situation which wouldn't come up in personal experimentation.

The following references, combined with a bit of personal exploration, will provide the concerned user with his/her own basis for decision.

A.E. Guedel, **Inhalation Anesthesia**, Macmillan, 1937
F.W. Clement, **Nitrous Oxide-Oxygen Anesthesia**, Lea and Febiger, 1951
T.A.B. Harris, **Mode of Action of Anesthetics**, Livingstone, 1951
V. Keating, **Anesthetic Accidents**, Year Book Pub., Chicago, 1956
H.K. Beecher, **Physiology of Anesthesia**, Oxford U. Press, 1938
C.L. Burstein, **Fundamental Considerations in Anesthesia**, Macmillan, 1949

Don't trust your family doctor about gas any more than you would trust him about LSD. He will respond on cue to one of the most elitist and firmly entrenched of all medical myths: that nitrous oxide will cause immediate incapacity or death if not administered in precisely the correct way. We have auto-administered nitrous oxide in all of the wrong ways for years, and our survival has led us to reject the severity of the medical warnings and to voice an alternative to the traditional medical proscriptions.

To avoid the hazards involved in nitrous oxide inhalation, the EBCPS has formulated several safety precautions. The main danger is that the user will render himself "unconscious" and will continue to inhale pure nitrous without oxygen. This serious circumstance can be easily avoided: Never attach the source of the gas to the mouth or nose *under any conditions.* The safety valve in auto-administration is the fact that the source of the gas falls away when the user momentarily passes out, allowing him/her to breathe vital atmospheric air. If a flexible tube such as a garden hose is connected to the tank, three adverse conditions occur. First, undue pressure is put on the lungs by the rushing gas; second, the throat and lips can freeze; and third, only one person can hit on the gas at a time.

An extremely satisfying alternative to a direct hose approach is the balloon method. Large "party" or "weather" balloons are filled from the tank; the balloons become conveniently portable containers, can be passed like joints, and allow for simultaneous inhalation by a large group of persons. In addition, the balloon method wastes little gas.

The optimum physical environment for the inhalation of nitrous oxide is a *soft place* - cushions, mattresses, thick carpets, perhaps a fern meadow or a freshly plowed field. People occasionally fall or pitch about or slump heavily. If one finds it desirable to stand up or walk while inhaling, it is recommended that extreme caution be employed, and, if possible a partner be secured.

Nausea is periodically reported, and it is difficult to tell whether or not a full stomach contributes to such discomfort. It is recommended, however, that users avoid large meals directly before a gas session.

There are less technical problems if the tank is standing up — the liquid nitrous is farther from the valve, the freezing area on the tank is reduced.

Casual deep breathing between hits of gas is a healthy policy. This increases the amount of oxygen in the system.

Cigarettes are often dropped or miswielded under the influence, and frequently pop precious balloons.

Filling up a small enclosed area like a closet or a car with pure nitrous oxide can be lethal.

Nitrous oxide is safe if used sensibly. Take care of your brain.

NITROUS OXIDE AND THE SURREAL CONDITION
by Dora Kaplan

To understand the nitrous oxide experience is to rediscover Surrealism as formulated by Andre Breton in **Manifestoes of Surrealism.** "There is every reason to believe that it (Surrealism) acts on the mind very much as drugs do; like drugs, it creates a certain state of need and can push man to frightful revolts."

Immediately upon ingestion of the drug one experiences a numbing of the body, a gradual loss of all sensation. Synesthesia frequently occurs and hearing, an awareness of an electronic-like throbbing, is the last sense to disappear. Like nitrous oxide, Surrealism "bewilders sensation, it aids in the systematic derangement of the senses."

As more gas is inspired a loss of ego and subsequent sense of unity (the cosmos is one and interrelated) as experienced in a mystical state of consciousness is achieved. There is one sentence in particular in the **Manifestoes** that not only states a fundamental belief of the Surrealists but accurately describes this aspect of the nitrous oxide experience: "There is a certain point of the mind from which life and death, the real and the imaginary, the past and the future, the communicable and incommunicable, the high and low, cease being perceived as contradictions." This state of mind is so foreign to our limited, rational, everyday consciousness that it is difficult to recall, as a particularly revelatory dream is immediately forgotten. "In a waking state, man is the plaything of his memory. Memory alone arrogates to itself the right to excerpt from dreams, to ignore the transitions." There is no point of reference, no control exercised by reason or any aesthetic or moral code; no consciously arrived-at-codification. "Reason's role being limited to taking note of, and appreciating, the luminous phenomenon." This unity-flow one also experiences as an omniscient innocence-wisdom (Taoistic objectivity– disinterested love and admiration for the Being of the other) that is available to all, that encompasses both animate and inanimate matter, that waits for release in the collective-mythic unconscious.

The transformation of reality as we know it is complete. The interpretation of the transformation will be incomplete until we live in the reality of the transformation, or as Breton would suggest, the Surreal: The resolution of all altered states of consciousness, including dreams, and reality.

The peak of the nitrous oxide intoxication, experienced after passing out and before regaining consciousness, is dominated by involuntarily generated images. The surrealists would meet regularly each evening and submit themselves to a state of collective hallucination. Liberated from all petty preoccupations, they went into a waking trance (auto-hypnosis): a state in which the unconscious would dictate to them. It is the experience of these images or hallucinations—perceptions of objects with no external cause—that provides the basis of a comparison between Surrealism and nitrous oxide.

"The Surrealistic atmosphere created by psychic automatism (expressed through automatic writing, verbally or any other manner), which I have wanted to put within the reach of everyone, is especially conducive to the production of the most beautiful images. One can even go so far as to say that in this dizzying race the images appear like the only guideposts of the mind. By slow degrees the mind becomes convinced of the supreme reality of these images. At first limiting itself to submitting to them, it soon realizes that they flatter its reason, and increase its knowledge accordingly. The mind becomes aware of the limitless expanses wherein its desires are made manifest, where the pros and cons are constantly consumed, where its obscurity does not betray it. It goes forward, borne by these images which enrapture it, which scarcely leave it any time to blow upon the fire in its fingers. This is the most beautiful night of all, the lightning-filled night: day, compared to it, is night.

For me, their greatest virtue (the Surrealistic images), I must confess is the one that is arbitrary to the highest degree, the one that takes the longest time to translate into practical language, either because it contains an immense amount of seeming contradiction or because, presenting itself as something sensational, it seems to end weakly (because it suddenly closes the angle of its compass), or because it derives from itself a ridiculous formal justification, or because it is of a hallucinatory kind, or because it very naturally gives to the abstract the mask of the concrete, or the opposite, or because it implies the negation of some elementary physical property, or because it provokes laughter.

The images generated are total, i.e., the hallucination is complete. One occupies worlds which don't exist objectively, all of which seem real. An analogy to chaotic time travel is helpful. The voyager finds himself here in a forest with prehistoric insects, there in a cosmic womb as the star-child at the end of 2001: A Space Odyssey, an integral and transcendental part of the universe. When inhaling gas alone I often come out of my trance imagining the room to be full of people, usually friends with whom I have taken gas in the past. In this case the hallucination duplicated a past event from my life but it is most often fictitious. This re-creation of a past reality gives the impression of everything occurring in the present. Past and future have no meaning. Time is. The hallucination is but a moment of leaving and returning to existence.

Perhaps the most beneficial aspect of the gas experience is the personal "revelation" or insight. These confrontations with individual fears and problems occasionally are of such magnitude as to plummet the person into a nightmare of self-doubt and madness. Similar to L.S.D., the revelation can be magnified and distorted until it is uncontrollable. Unlike acid, this experience on gas is transitory, erasing itself with the next inhalation. Because the nitrous oxide facilitates the release of unconscious material it has great therapeutic value— providing profound changes in a person's value-belief system and self-image. Like Surrealism, gas "aims at the total recovery of our psychic force by a means which is nothing other than the dizzying descent into ourselves, the systematic illumination of hidden places and the progressive darkening of other places, the perpetual excursion into the mist of forbidden territory. . . "

I would like to once again quote Breton and what he considers to be the aims of Surrealism, and suggest that the nitrous oxide experience allows for similar achievements:

> "Surrealism attempted to provoke, from the intellectual and moral point of view, an attack of conscience . . . a special part of its function being to examine with a critical eye the notions of reality and unreality, reason and irrationality, reflection and impulse, knowledge and 'fatal' ignorance, usefulness and uselessness.
> "Encyclopedia Philosophy. Surrealism is based on the belief in the superior reality of certain forms of previously neglected associations, in the omnipotence of dream, in the disinterested play of thought. It tends to substitute itself for them in solving all the principal problems of life."

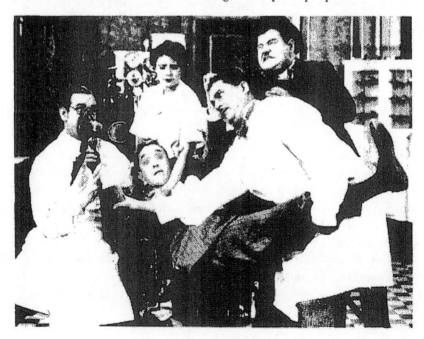

THE GUEDEL DUNKED DOG EXPERIMENT,

A 4-WAY DISCUSSION CONDUCTED UNDER
THE INFLUENCE OF NITROUS OXIDE, MAY 1970

M: I think we should discuss what kind of a tolerance we have to gas. I think we should note that we do housework under the influence, and can function almost normally after we've taken it for so many years. I'm interested in whether nitrous oxide benefits creative activity. Does it make one more creative? Do you think it frees creative channels? I know I personally feel that while nitrous breaks barriers and consciousness restrictions, that it doesn't really help when it comes to the creative process . . . in fact, I often have the fear that it destroys concentration and destroys brain cells, although I realize that that's a particular unconscious fear . . . It's hard for us to describe nitrous oxide because of how used we are to it. Now, when I take a single hit and sit back and try to describe the experience, I don't feel all that different from normal. I have never thought that doing gas in the daytime was all that different than doing it at night. It doesn't really matter . . .

I think nitrous oxide can overcome most of the feelings of fatigue. One of the things I know about nitrous oxide in me is that it seems to create a tremendous impatience that quite often impels me not only back toward the gas, but with other aspects of my usual environment, if I'm impatient with something, I'm even more impatient with it under the influence of gas. This is usually when I'm coming down from a gas rush, not during the peak of it. When I'm returning to normal consciousness . . .

D: Around the time of the fifth balloon, I reached a peak, almost . . . Like maintaining the high, maintaining the vibratory thing . . . It wasn't like that complete world, it was like vibrations of that world, it was like vibrations of that world maintained for five or ten minutes . . .

M: Have you ever passed out? Oh, you haven't passed out either. . . Well, you can pass out from one balloon by simply continuing to breathe it in and out like you would breathe air rather than doing it the way we're doing it and passing it like a joint.

S: It's right before you pass out that you get the most intense feeling.

J: This is really nice. . .

S: It's like being transported to a completely different reality.

M: You'll find out that this is consciousness too. . . They tell us you're either conscious or you're unconscious, but we find that that's not true. One of the things it does is make your voice deeper.
  How would you describe it in terms of an acid rush?

J: It appears to me to be completely different, as removed as it can be from an acid rush.

M: Are you more in tune with your own feelings under gas, or acid? Like things that you usually suppress. . .

J: Anything that I would suppress with acid, I seem to go right down to it, my mind goes right to it. . . With acid, I could be concerned with that part of me, with gas, that part of me seems just to arise in me. . .

M: Like revelations? Do you experience revelations?

J: A lot of joy.

S: I think revelations and hallucinations come with a lot of gas, similar effects to acid, too, after doing it for a long time.

M: I don't think it makes any difference if you do it for hours or just a couple of breaths, the effects can be the same. You can achieve the pass-out, total, ultimate effect from a single balloon.

S: It seems to me there are long term effects too. More similar to acid, like the room being constantly in motion, objects being constantly in motion, sensing their motion, and geometric patterns. . .

J: One of the differences is that on acid I go down to it, and on gas it comes up to me. On acid, it's hard to follow what someone is saying, 'cause I'm thinking about what I'm feeling, but here I'm very interested in what everyone else is 41 saying, so inhibitions are more erased than they are put in a place where I can be aware of them. On acid I can be aware of the inhibitions, here they're simply negligible.

M: I agree. Like some of the things we have done under the influence exhibited an extreme unawareness of other people being there, whether it be getting really greedy or flying across the room. . . and awareness of normal social etiquette and social consciousness seems to fall away and people run around and lie on the floor in a big pile, like happened to us in Berkeley. I think it's good that it breaks that down, normal cocktail party etiquette.

S: When you say that those things are negligible, do you mean that gas allows you to get to something higher?

J: Yeah, yeah. . . There's a bigger sense of fullness, on acid. . . not more than gas, but more than when you're straight. . . because you can examine those things and deal with them. . .

M: Do you experience any kind of mystical consciousness under gas?

S: That higher plane. . . is that unity and oneness?

M: Dave, how would you compare gas to meditating?

D: Like yesterday I compared it to om. Meditating is more of a peaceful thing for me and gas is more of a vibratory, turbulent thing. Like I thought it was every sound that reverberates from gas, but it's every impulse, it's not just the sound. Like any impulse my body takes in, gas will reverberate, whether it be like seeing something, hearing something, feeling something or thinking something. It's like a repetition trip, like ta-ta-ta-ta-ta-ta. It's like feeling the rhythm, being part of the rhythm, like locking into the rhythm in yourself and in the universe.

M: Is that the first time you passed out? What was it like? Was it like passing out on other drugs? Was it like going to sleep? Was it like dying?

D: It was really nice, actually. It was like another layer, another dimension added on to whatever state my consciousness was in.

M: Have you ever experienced this kind of consciousness before? Like through meditation or dreams?

D: No, not really. The closest thing is like I mentioned—oming. One time I was out on the beach, and the sound came out for a minute and a half after my breath had run out. The effect that it had was like this. All the world around me was similar to this—just a superheavy vibratory thing, a centering with the universe at the same time.

M: What kind of a trance are you in? See if you can explain it. Is this what people normally mean when they say 'pass out'?

J: My muscles were relaxed, they had quit working. My body felt closed.

S: Did you forget your body?

J: It just wouldn't work, so there's no sense in paying any attention to it.

M: Did you still feel you were Jacques F. sitting here with four people? Or did you tend to discard that?

J: It just wasn't a point of consideration. There was awareness of something. . .

M: Did you feel self-conscious? Did it bother you that you simply slumped over and passed out right here in front of the four of us?

J: Oh, no.

M: Did you feel a part of the great unity?

J: Yes, I did. I felt that I could take the same point, but it's from a different. . . like from having other drugs, the same specific thing I would talk about in different terms. Like the unity part of it is a very important thing, more than with other drugs.

J: As relating it to the other part of life, the non-drug part of life, I can't imagine. It's a very important drug.

M: Does it relate to the so-called "Eastern" concept, Mysticism? That thing that people don't usually deal with here in the continental United States. . . Do you think it affords you a mystical consciousness? Does it make you feel serene?

D: It's a definite centering thing, you know, center, you know, right in the middle, yeah, I just don't have. . . I relate it more to me than a philosophy thing. It seems personal. It kind of turns me on to my own vibratory level, it seems very familiar.

M: Do you feel more in touch with yourself?

D: No, under gas it's more of a vibratory thing with myself and my surroundings, rather than like an introspective trip. . . It seems much more like being in a perfect rhythmic sphere. . . a mantra is like a rhythmic bubble that you're inside of, that's perfect and that's affecting you.

J: That's what I meant when I said that I don't go down and think about it like on acid. On acid, you know, I go down and think about inhibitions or the globs beneath the surface and think about it, but. . .

M: Do you feel that anything wells up from your unconscious when you take gas? That happens to me. That has been reported. It's like dreams or the hypnogogic state.

J: I could certainly. . . that might have happened already. . . I can certainly see the possibility of that happening. . .

M: Did it make you want to laugh or smile?

J: Oh, yeah, I've been smiling a lot. . .

S: How do you think gas relates to society and to the social situation of civilization in general? And laws, authority, governments?

M: Say, in comparison to dreams which might be anti-authority and anti-government, dreams that reject all that that's outside there? Does it have anything to do with dreams? Do you have dream-like visions on gas?

M: What I love about gas is that it points out how absurd all this bullshit is. Trying to intellectualize about things, trying to think about things.

J: It seems to me to be a completely different direction, it's hard to compare it to dreams or acid. How do you connect it to the social situation?

M: Some people pass out and reject the entire social condition. We're still keeping a social situation. It seems to me if we each had a balloon and we're thinking about this as an exhilarant and not as a dope and getting really high that we'd react completely differently. We'd be off in our own complete trip, away from this social consciousness, we're all sitting up for example. That's very unnatural under the influence of nitrous oxide.

S: No, it seems to be that that is a condition of the furnishings of the apartment. But what about laws? Yeah, you reject the social condition but do you reject governmental laws? I do, but I wonder if this has anything to do with nitrous oxide. Does gas create an anarchistic frame of reference?

M: Yeah, we've all experienced non-verbalization of the experience. We've taken tape recorders into rooms and tried to speak into them and free associate and tell what was coming into our heads on gas and we found it couldn't be verbalized.

M: J, you appear to be smiling, why are you smiling? You appeared to have been in an unconscious condition.

J: No, not in an unconscious condition, there seems to be a self the whole time. There's always a self but it just gets smaller and it can just relate to itself with rhythms and music.

M: What do you mean by a self? One of the things I experience is loss of self, complete loss of identity and mixture and sort of blending into everything.

S: It seems to me that you experience less and less self until there's none.

M: Do you think that by a self that there's consciousness because I always experience that the last thing left is consciousness, which sort of equals energy, and consciousness is quantum energy just like an object, and we just become like, we can adopt in many instances the consciousnesses of objects around us.

J: We're just trying to identify something which at some time we related to and while taking gas we find it's the only thing that we find. There's a difference between unconsciousness and deep sleep or obliteration. There's something in me that stays on gas that goes when I'm in deep sleep.

M: Is it a pleasurable experience? Do you think that it's inferior to normal consciousness or superior, or is it more fun than being in deep sleep?

45

J: It's more joyous. I don't know whether it's inferior or superior but I would prefer to be joyous.

M: Do you have the feeling that it is an unnatural high or that you're screwing yourself up by putting chemicals into your body? Or that it's just an air and much safer to breathe than the smog?

J: Well, I've come from a drug thing and that's all irrelevant whether it's doing damage.

S: Yeah, I've experienced the same joy too, especially I experience a continuum of less and less self-consciousness and self-awareness and awareness of the outside world and then I feel complete loss of body and then I just have intimations of this, where there is a pure state of mind, a pure state of being that is sort of all-knowing, all-seeing and joyous and I exist as that kind of consciousness and that's all.

M: Is it like you become an omniscient and omnipresent thing?

S: Yes.

M: Yes, and Benjamin Blood talks about it in terms of "God" and we don't think in terms of god so we don't talk about it. We talk in terms of us becoming that sort of thing, that so-called god.

S: Yeah, divinity.

M: Yes, divinity, religiosity. They've dropped gas on spiders and injected it into animals. . . But we've asked doctors, we used to be into the trip of going to doctors and asking them about gas, but after a while we weren't getting any new information, and a lot of wrong information, and we ended up telling them things. Because we'd read the same books, only we had some 400,000 quarts of experience by ourselves, and we knew that a lot of the stuff we read in the books was bullshit. . . it said you're gonna die immediately if you do gas without an anesthetist hovering over you checking every breath, which is fine for hospitals, but we've been doing it for two and a half years and we're still functioning, in a manner of speaking, and they told us we were gonna be dead after three minutes.... When you passed out, did you experience anything that was like a dream? Did you have "visions?"

46

J: I felt like I was bordering, but that there was still perception, and it was a very slowed-down perception. . . a note-to-note perception of the music that was on. It was like clinging from note to note. . .

M: All right, that is what you were hearing, but what was your mind conceiving? What were you thinking of?

J: My mind was thinking of clinging from one note to the next note.

M: I fail to understand why the two of us report visions and you two do not report visions (referring to J. and D.).

J: Except perhaps that you go to movies and we listen to records... I don't relate to visions as much as I do to music, my mind moves in more musical patterns. There's perhaps a different scheme of consciousness if you think in sounds. . .

S: How does gas affect your sense of time? You've been under the influence about an hour and a half, does it seem like that to you?

D: It doesn't seem like it was an hour and a half, but each impulse seems to be prolonged. . . it's weird. . . it doesn't seem like I've been here for a long time, yet each moment is prolonged.

M: Do you have any hallucinations, the kind you might associate with too little oxygen, or too much?

J: I don't seem to be having any hallucinations. A lot of illusions, though, a lot of things that play on reality, nothing that seems to be made up separately from reality. Deviations and plays on themes. . .

M: Is gas like dying?

D: I don't know what dying is like, but I've had other things that were more like death trips.

M: Do you think gas can be used for self-improvement?

D: Well, for me its's not just insight after insight. I think the initial thing that you can learn from it can be learned from the first rush. The initial rush turned me on to a. . . I guess a universal vibratory thing.

47

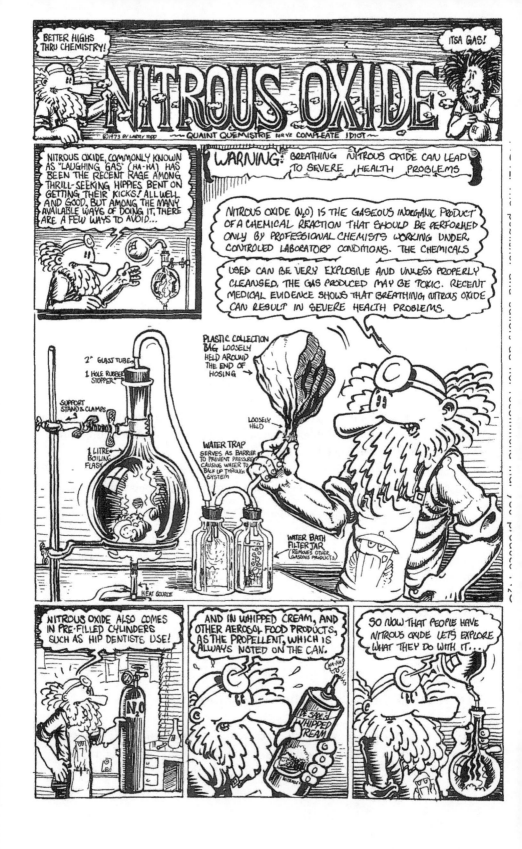

Stuart's Useful Information for the People, No. 12,

Being No. 4, of the

CHEMICAL EXPERIMENTALIST.

131.   BREATHING INTOXICATING GAS.

By permission, from the large Print published by Messrs Agnew & Zanetti

SIR HUMPHREY DAVY, BART P.R.S.

FISHER, SON & C? LONDON 1829.

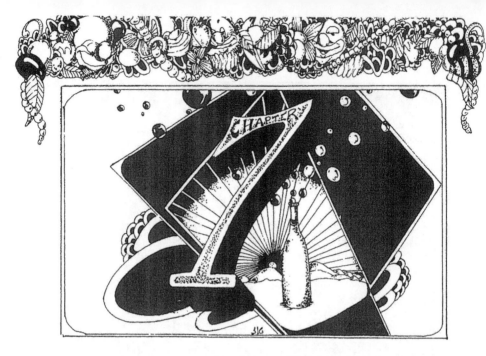

HUMPHREY DAVY ON LAUGHING GAS (1799)

From Humphry Davy's "Researches Chemical and/Philosophical"

RESEARCH IV

Relating to the effects produced by the respiration of nitrous oxide upon different individuals

Division I

History of the discovery -- effects produced by the respiration of different gases.

A short time after I began the study of Chemistry, in March 1798, my attention was directed to the dephlogisticated nitrous gas of Priestley, by Dr. Mitchill's Theory of Contagion.*

The fallacy of this theory was soon demonstrated, by a few coarse experiments made on small quantities of the gas procured from zinc and diluted nitrous acid. Wounds were exposed to its action, the bodies of animals were immersed in it without injury; and I breathed it mingled in small quantities with common air, without remarkable effects. An inability to procure it in sufficient quantities, prevented me at htis time from pursuing the experiments to any greater extent. I communicated an account of them to Dr. Beddoes.

---

* Dr. Mitchell attempted to prove from some phenomenon connected with contagious diseases, that dephlogisticated nitrous gas which he called oxide of septon, was the principle of contagion, and capable of producing the most terrible effects when respired by animals in the minutest quantities, or even when applied to the skin of muscular fibre.

In 1799, my situation in the Medical Pneumatic Institution, made it my duty to investigate the physiological effects of the aeriform fluids, the properties of which presented a chance of useful energy. At this period I recommenced the investigation.

A considerable time elapsed before I was able to procure the gas in a state of purity, and my first experiments were made on the mixtures of nitrous oxide, nitrogen and nitrous gas, which are produced during metallic solutions.

In the beginning of March, I prepared a large quantity of impure nitrous oxide from the nitrous solution of zinc. Of this I often breathed the quantities of a quart and two quarts generally mingled with more than equal parts of oxygen or common air. In the most decisive of those trials, its effects appeared to be depressing, and I imagined that it produced a tendency to fainting: the pulse was certainly rendered slower under its operation.

At his time, Mr. Southey respired it in an highly diluted state; it occassioned a slight degree of giddiness, and considerably diminished the quickness of his pulse.

Mr. C. Coates likewise respired it highly diluted, with similar effects.

In April, I obtained nitrous oxide in a state of purity, and ascertained many of its chemical properties. Reflections upon these properties and upon the former trials, made me resolve to endeavour to inspire it in its pure form, for I saw no other way in which its respirability or powers could be determined.*

I was aware of the danger of this experiment. It certainly would never have been made if the hypothesis of Dr. Mitchill had in the least influenced my mind. I thought that the effects might be possibly depressing and painful, but there were many reasons which induced me to believe that a single inspiration of a gas apparently possessing no immediate action on the irritable fibre, could neither destroy nor immediately injure the powers of life.

On April 11th, I made the first inspiration of pure nitrous oxide; it passed into the bronchia without stimulating the glottis, and produced no uneasy feeling in the lungs.

The result of this experiment proved that the gas was respirable, and induced me to believe that a farther trial of its effects might be made without danger.

On April 16th, Dr. Kinglake being accidentally present, I breathed three quarts of nitrous oxide from and into a silk bag for more than half a minute, without previously closing my nose or exhausting my lungs.

The first inspirations occasioned a slight degree of giddiness. This was succeeded by an uncommon sense of fulness of the head, accompanied with loss of distinct sensation and voluntary power, a feeling analogous to that

*I did not attempt to experiment upon animals, because they die nearly in equal times in non-respirable gases, and gases incapable of supporting life and possessed of no action on the venous blood.

produced in the first stage of intoxication; but unattended by pleasurable sensation. Dr. Kinglake, who felt my pulse, informed me that it was rendered quicker and fuller.

This trial did not satisfy me with regard to its powers; comparing it with the former ones I was unable to determine whether the operation was stimulant or depressing.

I communicated the results to Dr. Beddoes, and on April the 17th, he was present, when the following experiment was made.

Having previously closed my nostrils and exhausted my lungs, I breathed four quarts of nitrous oxide from and into a silk bag. The first feelings were similar to those produced in the last experiment; but in less than half a minute, the respiration being continued, they diminished gradually, and were succeeded by a sensation analogous to gentle pressure on all the muscles, attended by a highly pleasurable thrilling, particularly in the chest and the extremities. The objects around me became dazzling and my hearing more acute.   Towards the last inspirations, the thrilling increased, the sense of muscular power became greater, and at last an irresistible propensity to action was indulged in; I recollect but indistinctly what followed; I know that my motions were various and violent.

These effects very soon ceased after respiration. In ten minutes, I had recovered my natural state of mind. The thrilling in the extremities, continued longer than the other sensations. *

This experiment was made in the morning; no languor or exhaustion was consequent, my feelings throughout the day were as usual, and I passed the night in undisturbed repose.

The next morning the recollections of the effects of the gas were very indistinct, and had not remarks written immediately after the experiment recalled them to my mind, I should have even doubted their reality. I was willing indeed to attribute some of the strong emotion to the enthusiasm, which I supposed must have been necessarily connected with the perception of agreeable feelings, when I was prepared to experience painful sensations. Two experiments, however, made in the course of this day, with scepticism, convinced me that the effects were solely owing to the specific operation of the gas.

In each of them I breathed five quarts of nitrous oxide for rather a longer time than before. The sensations produced were similar, perhaps not quite so pleasurable; the muscular motions were much less violent.

Having thus ascertained the powers of the gas, I made many experiments to ascertain the length of time for which it might be breathed safely, its effects on the pulse, and its general effects on the health when often respired.

*Dr. Beddoes has given some account of this experiment, in his "Notice of Some Observations made at the Medical Pneumatic Institution." It was noticed in Mr. Nicholson's Phil. Journal for May 1799.

I found that I could breathe nine quarts of nitrous oxide for three minutes, and twelve quarts for rather more than four. I could never breathe it in any quantity, so long as five minutes. Whenever its operation was carried to the highest extent, the pleasurable thrilling at its height about the middle of the experiment, gradually diminished; the sense of pressure on the muscles was lost; impressions ceased to be perceived; vivid ideas passed rapidly through the mind, and voluntary power was altogether destroyed, so that the mouth-piece generally dropped from my unclosed lips.

Whenever the gas was in a high state of purity, it tasted distinctly sweet to the tongue and the palate, and had an agreeable odour. I often thought that it produced a feeling somewhat analogous to taste, in its application to my lungs. In one or two experiments, I perceived a distinct sense of warmth in my chest.

I never felt from it any thing like oppressive respiration: my inspirations became deep in proportion as I breathed it longer; but this phenomenon arose from increased energy of the muscles of respiration, and from a desire of increasing the pleasurable feelings.

Generally when I breathed from six to seven quarts, muscular motions were produced to a certain extent; sometimes I manifested my pleasure by stamping or laughing only; at other times, by dancing round the room and vociferating.

After the respiration of small doses, the exhilaration generally lasted for five or six minutes only. In one or two experiments when ten quarts had been breathed for near four minutes, an exhilaration and a sense of slight intoxication lasted for two or three hours.

On May 3d, to ascertain whether the gas would accelerate or retard the progress of sleep, I breathed at about 8 o'clock in the evening, 25 quarts of nitrous oxide, in quantities of six at a time, allowing but short intervals between each dose. The feelings were much less pleasurable than usual, and during the consumption of the two last doses, almost indifferent; indeed the gas was breathed rather too soon after its production, and contained some suspended acid vapour which stimulated the lungs so as to induce coughing.

After the experiments, for the first time I was somewhat depressed and debilitated; my propensity to sleep, however, came on at the usual hour, and as usual was indulged in, my repose was sound and unbroken.

Between May and July, I habitually breathed the gas, occassionally three or four times a day for a week together; at other periods, four or five times a week only.

The doses were generally from six to nine quarts; their effects appeared undiminished by habit, and were hardly ever exactly similar. Sometimes I had the feeling of intense intoxication, attended with but little pleasure; at other times, sublime emotions connected with highly vivid ideas; my pulse was generally increased in fulness, but rarely in velocity.   57

GILLRAY'S DRAWING OF HUMPHRY DAVY LECTURING AT THE ROYAL INSTITUTION, JUNE 20TH, 1801. Sir Davy is holding the bellows. He was in London giving a series of lectures on Pneumatic Chemistry, and he dispensed nitrous oxide to members of the audience who wanted to try it. The *Philosophical Magazine* took note of the event: "Mr. Underwood experienced so much pleasure from breathing it that he lost all sense of everything else, and the breathing bag could only be taken from him at last by force." (H. Bence-Jones, *The Royal Institution*.) This lecture appears to be Davy's last work with nitrous oxide.

The general effects of its operation, upon my health and state of mind, are extremely difficult of description; nor can I well discriminate between its agency and that of other physical and moral causes.

I slept much less than usual, and previous to sleep, my mind was long occupied by visible imagery. I had a constant desire of action, a restlessness, and an uneasy feeling about the praecordia analogous to the sickness of hope.

But perhaps these phenomena in some measure depended on the interest and labour connected with the experimental investigation relating to the production of nitrous oxide, by which I was at this time incessantly occupied.

My appetite was as usual and my pulse not materially altered. Sometimes for an hour after the inspiration of the gas, I experienced a species of mental indolence* pleasing rather than otherwise, and never ending in listlessness.

During the last week in which I breathed it uniformly, I imagined that I had increased sensibility of touch: my fingers were pained by any thing rough and the tooth edge produced from slighter causes than usual. I was certainly more irritable, and felt more acutely from trifling circumstances. My bodily strength was rather diminished than increased.

At the end of July, I left off my habitual course of respiration; but I continued occasionally to breathe the gas, either for the sake of enjoyment, or with a view of ascertaining its operations under particular circumstances.

In one instance, when I had head-ache from indigestion, it was immediately removed by the effects of a large dose of gas; though it afterwards returned but with much less violence. In a second instance, a slighter degree of head-ache was wholly removed by two doses of gas.

The power of the immediate operation of the gas in removing intense physical pain, I had a very good opportunity for ascertaining.

In cutting one of the unlucky teeth called dentes sapientiae, I experienced an extensive inflammation of the gum, accompanied with great pain, which equally destroyed the power of repose, and of consistent action.

On the day when the inflammation was the most troublesome, I breathed three doses of nitrous oxide. The pain always diminished after the first four or five inspirations; the thrilling came on as usual, and uneasiness was for a few minutes swallowed up in pleasure. As the former state of mind however returned, the state of organ returned with it; and I once imagined that the pain was more severe after the experiment than before.

* *Mild physical pleasure is perhaps always destructive to action. Almost all our powerful voluntary actions, arise either from hope, fear, or desire; and the most powerful from desire, which is an emotion produced by the coalescence of hope or ideal pleasure with physical pain.*   59

In August, I made many experiments with a view of ascertaining whether any analogy existed between the sensible effects of the different gases which are sooner or later fatal to life when respired, and those of nitrous oxide.

I respired four quarts of hydrogen* nearly pure, produced from zinc and muriatic acid, for near a minute, my lungs being previously exhausted and my nostrils carefully closed. The first six or seven inspirations produced no sensations whatever: in half a minute I perceived a disagreeable oppression of the chest, which obliged me to respire very quickly; this oppression gradually increased, till at last the pain of suffocation compelled me to leave off breathing. I felt no giddiness during or after the experiment; my pulse was rendered feebler and quicker; and a by-stander informed me that towards the last, my cheeks became purple.

In a second experiment, when the hydrogen was produced from iron and diluted sulphuric acid, I was unable to respire it for so long as three quarters of a minute; a transient giddiness and muscular debility were produced, the pulse was rendered very feeble, and the pain of suffocation was greater than before.

I breathed three quarts of nitrogen mingled with a very small portion of carbonic acid, for near a minute. It produced no alteration in my sensations for the first twenty seconds: then the painful sense of suffocation gradually came on, and increased rapidly in the last quarter of the minute, so as to oblige me to desist from the experiment. My pulse was rendered feebler and quicker. I felt no affection whatever in the head.

Mr. Watt's observations on the respiration of diluted hydrocarbonate by men and Dr. Beddoe's experiments on the destruction of animals by pure hydrocarbonate, proved that its effects were highly deleterious.

As it destroyed life apparently by rendering the muscular fibre inirritable without producing any previous excitment, I was anxious to compare its sensible effects with those of nitrous oxide, which at this time I believed to destroy life by producing the highest possible excitement, ending in lesion of organization.

In the first experiment, I breathed for near a minute three quarts of hydrocarbonate mingled with nearly two quarts of atmospheric air.† It produced a slight giddiness and pain in the head, and a momentary loss of voluntary power: my pulse was rendered much quicker and feebler. These effects, however, went off in five minutes, and I had no return of giddiness.

Emboldened by this trial, in which the feelings were not unlike those I experienced in the first experiments on nitrous oxide, I resolved to breathe pure hydrocarbonate.

* Pure hydrogen has been often respired by different philosophers, particularly by Scheele, Fontana, and the adventurous and unfortunate Rosier.

† I believe it had never been breathed before by any individual, in a state so little diluted.

For this purpose, I introduced into a silk bag four quarts of gas nearly pure, which was carefully produced from the decomposition of water by charcoal an hour before, and which had a very strong and disagreeable smell.

My friend, Mr. James Tobin, Jun. being present, after a forced exhaustion of my lungs, the nose being accurately closed, I made three inspirations and expirations of the hydrocarbonate. The first inspiration produced a sort of numbness and loss of feeling in the chest and about the pectoral muscles. After the second inspiration, I lost all power of perceiving external things, and had no distinct sensation except a terrible oppression on the chest. During the third expiration, this feeling disappeared, I seemed sinking into annihilation, and had just power enough to drop the mouth piece from my unclosed lips. A short interval must have passed during which I respired common air, before the objects about me were distinguishable. On recollecting myself, I faintly articulated, "I do not think I shall die." Putting my finger on the wrist, I found my pulse thread-like and beating with excessive quickness.

In less than a minute, I was able to walk, and the painful oppression on the chest directed me to open air.

After making a few steps which carried me to the garden, my head became giddy, my knees trembled, and I had just sufficient voluntary power to throw myself on the grass. Here the painful feeling of the chest increased with such violence as to threaten suffocation. At this moment I asked for some nitrous oxide. Mr. Dwyer brought me a mixture of oxygen and nitrous oxide. I breathed this for a minute, and believed myself relieved. In five minutes, the painful feelings began gradually to diminish. In an hour they had nearly disappeared, and I felt only excessive weakness and a slight swimming of the head. My voice was very feeble and indistinct. This was at two o'clock in the afternoon.

I afterwards walked slowly for about half an hour, with Mr. Tobin, Jun. and on my return, was so much stronger and better, as to believe that the effects of the gas had disappeared; though my pulse was 120, and very feeble. I continued without pain for near three quarters of an hour, when the giddiness returned with such violence as to oblige me to lie on the bed; it was accompanied with nausea, loss of memory, and deficient sensation. In about an hour and half, the giddiness went off, and was succeeded by an excruciating pain in the forehead and between the eyes, with transient pains in the chest and extremities.

Towards night these affections gradually diminished. At ten,* no disagreeable feeling except weakness remained. I slept sound, and awoke in the morning very feeble and very hungry. No recurrence of the symptoms took place, and I had nearly recovered my strength by the evening.

· I have been minute in the account of this experiment, because it proves, that hydrocarbonate acts as a sedative, i.e. that it produces diminution of vital

* I ought to observe that between eight and ten, I took, by the advice of Dr. Beddoes, two or three doses of diluted nitric acid.

action, and debility, without previously exciting. There is every reason to believe, that if I had taken four or five inspirations instead of three, they would have destroyed life immediately without producing any painful sensation. Perhaps most of the uneasy feelings after the experiment, were connected with the return of the healthy condition of organs.†

About a week after this experiment, I attempted to respire carbonic acid, not being at the time acquainted with the experiments of Rosier.

I introduced into a silk bag four quarts of well washed carbonic acid produced from carbonate of ammonia* by heat, and after a complete voluntary exhaustion of my lungs, attempted to inspire it. It tasted strongly acid in the mouth and fauces, and produced a sense of burning at the top of the uvula. In vain I made powerful voluntary efforts to draw it into the windpipe; at the moment that the epiglottis was raised a little, a painful stimulation was introduced, so as to close it spasmodically on the glottis; and thus in repeated trials I was prevented from taking a single particle of carbonic acid into my lungs.

I tried to breathe a mixture of two quarts of common air and three of carbonic acid, without success; it stimulated the epiglottis nearly in the same manner as pure carbonic acid, and was perfectly non-respirable.

I found that a mixture of three quarts of carbonic acid with seven of common air was respirable, I breathed it for near a minute. At the time, it produced a slight degree of giddiness, and an inclination to sleep. These effects, however, very rapidly disappeared after I had ceased to breathe† and no other affections followed.

During the course of experiments on nitrous oxide, I several times breathed oxygen procured from manganese by heat, for from three to five minutes.

In respiring eight or ten quarts; for the first two or three minutes I could perceive no effects. Towards the end, even when I breathed very slowly, my respiration became oppressed, and I felt a sensation analogous to that produced by the want of fresh air; though but little of the oxygen had been consumed.

---

† *By whatever cause the exhaustion of organs is produced, pain is almost uniformly connected with their returning health. Pain is rarely ever perceived in limbs debilitated by fatigue till after they have been for some hours at rest. Pain is uniformly connected with the recovery from the debility induced by Typhus, often with the recovery from that produced by the stimulation of opium and alcohol.*

Carbonic acid is produced in this way in a high state of purity, and with great readiness.

† *Carbonic acid possesses no action on arterial blood. Hence perhaps its slight effects when breathed mingled with large quantities of common air. Its effects are very marked upon venous blood! If it were thrown forcibly into the lungs of animals, the momentary application of it to the pulmonary venous blood would probably destroy life.*   62

In one experiment when I breathed from and into a bag containing 20 quarts of oxygen for nearly six minutes, Dr. Kinglake felt my pulse, and found it not altered in velocity, but rather harder than before. I perceived no effects but those of oppression on the chest. *

Having observed in my experiments upon venous blood, that nitrous gas rendered that fluid of a purple tinge, very like the colour generated in it by nitrous oxide; and finding no painful effects produced by the application of nitrous gas to the bare muscular fibre, I began to imagine that this gas might be breathed with impunity, provided it were possible in any way to free the lungs of common air before inspiration, so as to prevent the formation of nitrous acid.

On this supposition, during a fit of enthusiasm produced by the respiration of nitrous oxide, I resolved to endeavour to breathe nitrous gas. 114 cubic inches of nitrous gas were introduced into the large mercurial airholder; two small silk bags of the capacity of seven quarts were filled with nitrous oxide.

After a forced exhaustion of my lungs, my nose being accurately closed, I made three inspirations and expirations of nitrous oxide in one of the bags, to free my lungs as much as possible from atmospheric oxygen; then, after a full expiration of the nitrous oxide, I transferred my mouth from the mouth-piece of the bag to that of the air-holder, and turning the stop-cock, attempted to inspire the nitrous gas. In passing through my mouth and fauces, it tasted astringent and highly disagreeable; it occasioned a sense of burning in the throat, and produced a spasm of the epiglottis so painful as to oblige me to desist instantly from attempts to inspire it. After moving my lips from the mouth-piece, when I opened them to inspire common air, aeriform nitrous acid was

* In a conversation with Mr. Watt, relating to the powers of gases, that excellent philosopher told me he had for some time entertained a suspicion, that the effects attributed to oxygen produced from manganese by heat, in some measure depended upon nitrous acid suspended in the gas, formed during ignition by the union of some of the oxygen of the manganese with nitrogen likewise condensed in it.

In the course of experiments on nitrous acid, detailed in Research I, made in September, October and December 1799, I several times experienced a severe oppression on the chest and difficulty of respiration, not unanalogous to that produced by oxygen, but much more violent, from breathing an atmosphere loaded with nitrous acid vapour. This fact seemed to confirm Mr. Watt's suspicion. I confess, however, that I have never been able to detect any smell of nitrous acid, either by means of my own organs or those of others, during the production of oxygen; when the gas is suffered to pass into the atmosphere. The oxygen breathed in the experiments detailed in the text, had been for some days in contact with water.

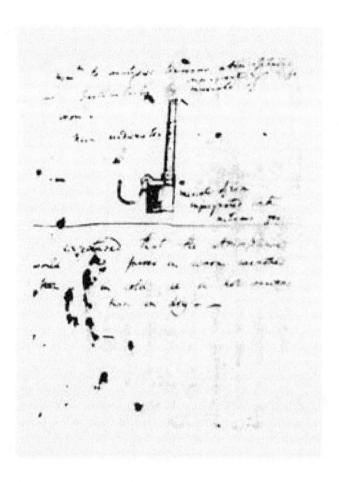

PAGE FROM HUMPHRY DAVY'S NOTEBOOK. On April 11, 1799, Humphry Davy made his first inspiration of pure nitrous oxide. He proceeded to experiment widely on himself, breathing in quantities of between six and nine quarts at a time. He gave the gas to his friends and prevailed upon them for written descriptions; he administered the gas to animals; he combined the gas with alcohol inebriation; he sat inside a nitrous oxide filled box for an hour and a half; he occasionally was observed dashing about his laboratory and falling to the floor. Sir Humphry also carried his experiments outside the laboratory. He reports, in his book *Researches Chemical and Philosophical*: "Whenever I have breathed the gas after excitement from moral or physical causes, the delight has been often intense and sublime."

instantly formed in my mouth, which burnt the tongue and palate, injured the teeth, and produced an inflammation of the mucous membrane which lasted some hours.

As after the respiration of nitrous oxide in the experiments in the last Research, a small portion of the residual atmospheric air remained in the lungs, mingled with the gas, after forced expiration; it is most probable that a minute portion of nitrous acid was formed in this experiment, when the nitrous gas was taken into the mouth and fauces, which might produce its stimulating properties. If so, perhaps I owe my life to the circumstance; for supposing I had taken an inspiration of nitrous gas, and even that it had produced no positive effects, it is highly improbable, that by breathing nitrous oxide, I should have freed my lungs from it, so as to have prevented the formulation of nitrous acid when I again inspired common air. I never design again to attempt so rash an experiment.

In the beginning of September I often respired nitrous oxide mingled with different proportions of common air or oxygen. The effects produced by the diluted gas were much less violent that those produced by pure nitrous oxide. They were generally pleasant: the thrilling was not often perceived, but a sense of exhilaration was almost constant.

Between September and the end of October, I made but few experiments on respiration, almost the whole of my time being devoted to chemical experiments on the production and analysis of nitrous oxide.

At this period my health being somewhat injured by the constant labour of experimenting, and the perpetual inhalation of the acid vapours of the laboratory, I went into Cornwall; where new associations of ideas and feelings, common exercise, a pure atmosphere, luxurious diet and moderate indulgence in wine, in a month restored me to health and vigour.

Nov. 27th; immediately after my return, being fatigued by a long journey, I respired nine quarts of nitrous oxide, having been precisely thirty-three days without breathing any. The feelings were different from those I had experienced in former experiments. After the first six or seven inspirations, I gradually began to lose the perception of external things, and a vivid and intense recollection of some former experiments passed through my mind, so that I called out "what an amazing concatenation of ideas!" I had no pleasurable feeling whatever, I used no muscular motion, nor did I feel any disposition to it; after a minute, when I made the note of the experiment, all the uncommon sensations had vanished; they were succeeded by a slight soreness in one of the arms and in the leg: in three minutes these affections likewise disappeared.

From this experiment I was inclined to suppose that my newly acquired health had diminished my susceptibility to the effects of the gas. About 10 days after, however, I had an opportunity of proving the fallacy of this supposition.

Immediately after a journey of 126 miles, in which I had no sleep the preceding night, being much exhausted, I respired seven quarts of gas for near three minutes. It produced the usual pleasurable effects, and slight muscular motion. I continued exhilarated for some minutes afterwards: but in half an hour found myself neither more nor less exhausted than before the experiment. I had a great propensity to sleep.

I repeated the experiment four or five times in the following week, with similar effects. My susceptibility was certainly diminished. I even thought that I was more affected than formerly by equal doses.

Though, except in one instance, when indeed the gas was impure, I had experienced no decisive exhaustion after excitement from nitrous oxide, yet still I was far from being satisfied that it was unanalogous to stimulants in general. No experiment had been made in which the excitement from nitrous oxide had been kept up for so great a length of time and carried to so great an extent as that in which it is uniformly succeeded by excessive debility under the agency of other powers.

It occurred to me, that supposing nitrous oxide to be a stimulant of the common class, it would follow that the debility produced in consequence of excessive stimulation by a known agent, ought to be *increased* after excitement from nitrous oxide.†

To ascertain whether this was the case, I made, on December 23rd, at four p.m. the following experiment. I drank a bottle of wine in large draughts in less than eight minutes. Whilst I was drinking, I perceived a sense of fulness in the head, and throbbing of the arteries, not unanalogous to that produced in the first stage of nitrous oxide excitement. After I had finished the bottle, this fulness increased, the objects around me became dazzling, the power of distinct articulation was lost, and I was unable to walk steadily. At this moment the sensations were rather pleasurable than otherwise, the sense of fulness in the head soon however increased so as to become painful, and in less than an hour I sunk into a state of insensibility.*

In this situation I must have remained for two hours or two hours and a half.

I was awakened by head-ache and painful nausea. The nausea continued even after the contents of the stomach had been ejected. The pain in the head every minute increased; I was neither feverish nor thirsty; my bodily and mental debility were excessive, and the pulse feeble and quick.

In this state I breathed for near a minute and half five quarts of gas, which was brought to me by the operator for nitrous oxide; but as it produced no

† In the same manner as the debility from intoxication by two bottles of wine is increased by a third.

* *I ought to observe that my usual drink is water, that I had been little accustomed to take wine or spirits, and have never been completely intoxicated but once before in the course of my life. This will account for the powerful effects of a single bottle of wine.*

sensations whatever, and apparently rather increased my debility, I am almost convinced that it was from some accident, either common air, or very impure nitrous oxide.

Immediately after this trial, I respired 12 quarts of oxygen for near four minutes. It produced no alteration in my sensations at the time; but immediately after I imagined that I was a little exhilarated.

The head-ache and debility still however continuing with violence, I examined some nitrous oxide which had been prepared in the morning, and finding it very pure, respired seven quarts of it for two minutes and half.

I was unconscious of head-ache after the third inspiration; the usual pleasurable thrilling was produced, voluntary power was destroyed, and vivid ideas rapidly passed through my mind; I made strides across the room, and continued for some minutes much exhilarated. Immediately after the exhilaration had disappeared, I felt a slight return of the head-ache; it was connected with transient nausea. After two minutes, when a small quantity of acidified wine had been thrown from the stomach, both the nausea and head-ache disappeared; but languor and depression not very different in degree from those existing before the experiment, succeeded. They, however, gradually went off before bed time. I slept sound the whole of the night except for a few minutes, during which I was kept awake by a trifling head-ache. In the morning, I had no longer any debility. No head-ache or giddiness came on after I had arisen, and my appetite was very great.

This experiment proved, that debility from intoxication was not increased by excitement from nitrous oxide. The head-ache and depression, it is probable, would have continued longer if it had not been administered. It is not likely that the slight nausea following the effects of the gas was produced by new excitability given to the stomach?

To ascertain with certainty, whether the most extensive action of nitrous oxide compatible with life, was capable of producing debility, I resolved to breathe the gas for such a time and in such quantities, as to produce excitement equal in duration and superior in intensity to that occasioned by high intoxication from opium or alcohol.

To habituate myself to the excitement, and to carry it on gradually, on December 26th, I was inclosed in an air-tight breathing box,† of the capacity of about 9 cubic feet and half, in the presence of Dr. Kinglake.

After I had taken a situation in which I could by means of a curved thermometer inserted under the arm, and a stop-watch, ascertain the alterations in my pulse and animal heat, 20 quarts of nitrous oxide were thrown into the box.

---

† *The plan of this box was communicated by Mr. Watt. An account of it will be detailed in the Researches.*

For three minutes I experienced no alteration in my sensations, though immediately after the introduction of the nitrous oxide the smell and taste of it were very evident.*

In four minutes I began to feel a slight glow in the cheeks, and a generally diffused warmth over the chest, though the temperature of the box was not quite 50°. I had neglected to feel my pulse before I went in; at this time it was 104 and hard, the animal heat was 98°. In ten minutes the animal heat was near 99°, in a quarter of an hour 99.5°, when the pulse was 102, and fuller than before.

At this period 20 quarts more of nitrous oxide were thrown into the box, and well mingled with the mass of air by agitation.

In 25 minutes the animal heat was 100°, pulse 124. In 30 minutes, 20 quarts more of gas were introduced.

My sensations were now pleasant; I had a generally diffused warmth without the slightest moisture of the skin, a sense of exhilaration similar to that produced by a small dose of wine, and a disposition to muscular motion and to merriment.

In three quarters of an hour the pulse was 104, and animal heat not quite 99.5°, the temperature of the chamber was 64°. The pleasurable feelings continued to increase, the pulse became fuller and slower, till in about an hour it was 88°, when the animal heat was 99°.

20 quarts more of air were admitted. I had now a great disposition to laugh; luminous points seemed frequently to pass before my eyes, my hearing was certainly more acute, and I felt a pleasant lightness and power of exertion in my muscles. In a short time the symptoms became stationary; breathing was rather oppressed, and on account of the great desire of action, rest was painful.

I now came out of the box, having been in precisely an hour and quarter.

The moment after, I began to respire 20 quarts of unmingled nitrous oxide. A thrilling, extending from the chest to the extremities, was almost immediately produced. I felt a sense of tangible extension highly pleasurable in every limb; my visible impressions were dazzling, and apparently magnified, I heard distinctly every sound in the room, and was perfectly aware of my situation.† By degrees, as the pleasurable sensations increased, I lost all connection with external things; trains of vivid visible images rapidly passed through my mind, and were connected with words in such a manner, as to produce perceptions perfectly novel. I existed in a world of newly connected and newly modified ideas. I theorised--I imagined that I made discoveries. When I was awakened from this semi-delirious trance by Dr. Kinglake, who took the bag

---

* *The nitrous oxide was diluted to act much; it was mingled with near 22 times its bulk of atmospheric air.*

† *In all these experiments, after the first minute, my cheeks became purple.*

from my mouth, indignation and pride were the first feelings produced by the sight of the persons about me. My emotions were enthusiastic and sublime; and for a minute I walked round the room, perfectly regardless of what was said to me. As I recovered my former state of mind, I felt an inclination to communicate the discoveries I had made during the experiment. I endeavoured to recall the ideas, they were feeble and indistinct; one collection of terms, however, presented itself: and with the most intense belief and prophetic manner, I exclaimed to Dr. Kinglake, *"Nothing exists but thoughts!--the universe is composed of impressions, ideas, pleasures and pains!"*

About three minutes and half only had elapsed during this experiment, though the time as measured by the relative vividness of the recollected ideas, appeared to me much longer.

Not more than half of the nitrous oxide was consumed. After a minute, before the thrilling of the extremities had disappeared, I breathed the remainder. Similar sensations were again produced; I was quickly thrown into the pleasurable trance, and continued in it longer than before. For many minutes after the experiment, I experienced the thrilling in the extremities, the exhilaration continued nearly two hours. For a much longer time I experienced the mild enjoyment before described connected with indolence; no depression or feebleness followed. I ate my dinner with great appetite and found myself lively and disposed to action immediately after. I passed the evening in executing experiments. At night I found myself unusually cheerful and active; and the hours between eleven and two, were spent in copying the foregoing detail from the common-place book, and in arranging the experiments. In bed I enjoyed profound repose. When I awoke in the morning, it was with consciousness of pleasurable existence, and this consciousness more or less continued through the day.

Since December, I have very often breathed nitrous oxide. My susceptibility to its power is rather increased than diminished. I find six quarts a full dose, and I am rarely able to respire it in any quantity for more than two minutes and half.

The mode of its operation is somewhat altered. It is indeed very different at different times.

I am scarcely ever excited into violent muscular action; the emotions are generally much less intense and sublime than in the former experiments, and not often connected with thrillings in the extremities.

When troubled with indigestion, I have been two or three times unpleasantly affected after the excitement of the gas. Cardialgia, eructations, and unpleasant fulness of the head were produced.

I have often felt very great pleasure when breathing it alone, in darkness and silence, occupied only by ideal existence. In two or three instances when I have breathed it amidst noise, the sense of hearing has been painfully affected even by moderate intensity of sound. The light of the sun has sometimes been

WORDS WRITTEN BY HUMPHRY DAVY WHILE UNDER THE
INFLUENCE OF NITROUS OXIDE. From a page of Davy's notebook.
Sir Humphry remarked, on more than one occasion, that it was difficult
for him to certify the precise accuracy of his experiments because the
exhilirating effects of the nitrous gas would disrupt his laboratory
activities.

disagreeably dazzling. I have once or twice felt an uneasy sense of tension in the cheeks and transient pains in the teeth.

Whenever I have breathed the gas after excitement from moral or physical causes, the delight has been often intense and sublime.

On May 5th, at night, after walking for an hour amidst the scenery of the Avon, at this period rendered exquisitely beautiful by bright moonshine; my mind being in a state of agreeable feeling, I respired six quarts of newly prepared nitrous oxide.

The thrilling was very rapidly produced. The objects around me were perfectly distinct, and the light of the candle not as usual dazzling. The pleasurable sensation was at first local, and perceived in the lips and about the cheeks. It gradually, however, diffused itself over the whole body, and in the middle of the experiment was for a moment so intense and pure as to absorb existence. At this moment, and not before, I lost consciousness; it was, however, quickly restored, and I endeavoured to make a by-stander acquainted with the pleasure I experienced by laughing and stamping. I had no vivid ideas. The thrilling and the pleasurable feeling continued for many minutes; I felt two hours afterwards, a slight recurrence of them, in the intermediate state between sleeping and waking; and I had during the whole of the night, vivid and agreeable dreams. I awoke in the morning with the feeling of restless energy, or that desire of action connected with no definite object, which I had often experienced in the course of experiments in 1799.

I have two or three times since respired nitrous oxide under similar circumstances; but never with equal pleasure.

During the last fortnight, I have breathed it very often; the effects have been powerful and the sensations uncommon; but pleasurable only in a slight degree.

I ought to have observed that a desire to breathe the gas is always awakened in me by the sight of a person breathing, or even by that of an air-bag or an air-holder.

I have this day, June 5th, respired four large doses of gas. The first two taken in the morning acted very powerfully; but produced no thrilling nor other pleasurable feelings. The effects of the third, breathed immediately after a hearty dinner, were pleasant, but neither intense nor intoxicating. The fourth was respired at night in darkness and silence after the occurrence of a circumstance which had produced some anxiety. This dose affected me powerfully and pleasantly; a slight thrilling in the extremities was produced; an exhilaration continued for some time, and I have had but little return of uneasiness; (11 p.m.)

From the nature of the language of feeling, the preceding detail contains many imperfections; I have endeavoured to give as accurate an account as possible of the strange effects of nitrous oxide, by making use of terms standing for the most similar common feelings.

We are incapable of recollecting pleasures and pains of sense.* It is impossible to reason concerning them, except by means of terms which have been associated with them at the moment of their existence, and which are afterwards called up amidst trains of concomitant ideas.

When pleasures or pains are new or connected with new ideas, they can never be intelligibly detailed unless associated during their existence with terms standing for analogous feelings.

I have sometimes experienced from nitrous oxide, sensations similar to no others, and they have consequently been indescribable. This has been likewise often the case with other persons. Of two paralytic patients who were asked what they felt after breathing nitrous oxide, the first answered, *"I do not know how, but very queer."* The second said, *"I felt like the sound of a harp."* Probably in the one case, no analogous feelings had ever occurred. In the other, the pleasurable thrillings were similar to the sensations produced by music; and hence, they were connected with terms formerly applied to music.

Physical pleasure and pain generally occur connected with a compound impression, i.e. an organ and some object. When the idea left by the compound impression, is called up by being linked accidentally to some other idea or impression, no recurrence, or the slightest possible, of the pleasure or pain in any form will take place. But when the compound impression itself exists without the physical pleasure or pain, it will awaken ideal or intellectual pleasure or pain, i.e. hope or fear. So that physical pleasure and pain are to hope and fear, what impressions are to ideas. For instance, assuming no accidental association, the child does not fear the fire before he is burnt. When he puts his finger to the fire he feels the physical pain of burning, which is connected with a visible compound impression, the fire and his finger. Now when the compound idea of the fire and his finger, left by the compound impression are called up by his mother, saying, "You have burnt your finger," nothing like fear or the pain of burning is connected with it. But when the finger is brought near the fire, i.e. when the compound impression again exists, the ideal pain of burning or the passion of fear is awakened, and it becomes connected with those very actions which removed the finger from the fire.

BENJAMIN PAUL BLOOD ON LAUGHING GAS (1874)

From **The Anesthetic Revelation and the Gist of Philosophy** *by Benjamin Paul Blood(1832 - 1919)Amsterdam, in N.Ÿ., America, 1874, p. 33-37.*

By the Anesthetic Revelation I mean a certain survived condition, (or uncondition) in which is the satisfaction of philosophy by an appreciation of the genius of being, which appreciation cannot be brought out of that condition into the normal sanity of sense -- cannot be formally remembered, but remains informal, forgotten until we return to it.

> *As here we find in trances, men*
> *Forget the dream that happens then,*
> *Until they fall in trance again.*

Of this condition, although it may have been attained otherwise, I know only by the use of anesthetic agents. After experiments ranging over nearly fourteen years I affirm -- what any man prove at will -- that there is an invariable and reliable condition (or uncondition) ensuing about the instant of recall from anaesthetic stupor to sensible observation, or "coming to," in which the genius of being is revealed; but because it cannot be remembered in the normal condition it is lost altogether through the infrequency of the anaesthetic treatment in any individual's case ordinarily, and buried, amid the hum of returning common sense, under the epitaph of all illumination "this is a queer world." Yet I have warned others to expect this wonder on entering the anaesthetic slumber, and none so cautioned has failed to report of it in terms which assured me of its realization. I have spoken with various persons also who. induce anesthesis professionally (dentists, surgeons, etc.,) who had observed that many patients at the moment of recall seem as having made a startling yet somehow matter-of-course (and even grotesque) discovery in their own nature, and try to speak of it, but invariably fail in a lost mood of introspection. Of what astonishes them it is hard to give or receive intimation; but I think most persons who have tested it will accept this as the central point of the illumination: That sanity is not the basic quality of intelligence, but it is a mere condition which is variable, and like the humming of a wheel, goes up or down the musical gamut according to a physical activity; and that only in sanity is formal or contrasting thought, while the naked life is realized only outside of sanity altogether; and it is the instant contrast of this "tasteless water of souls" with formal thought as we "come to", that leaves in the patient an astonishment that the awful mystery of Life is at last but a homely and a common thing, and that aside from mere formality the majestic and the absurd are of equal dignity. The astonishment is aggravated as at a thing of course, missed by sanity in over-stepping, as in too foreign a search, or with too eager an attention: as in finding one's spectacles on one's nose, or in making in the dark a step higher than the stair. My first experiences of this revelation had many varieties of emotion; but as a man grows calm and determined by experience in general, so am I now not only firm and familiar in this weird condition, but triumphant - divine. To minds of sanguine imagination there will be a sadness in the tenor of the mystery, as if the key-note of the Universe were low, -- for no poetry, no emotion known to the normal sanity of man can furnish a hint of its primeval prestige and its all but appalling solemnity; but for such as have felt sadly the instability of temporal things there is a comfort of serenity and ancient peace; while for the resolved and imperious spirit there are majesty and supremacy unspeakable. Nor can it be long until all who enter the anaesthetic condition (and there are hundreds every secular day) will be taught to expect this revelation, and will date from its experience their initiation into the secret of Life.

Men and brethren, into this prevading genius we pass, forgetting and forgotten, and thenceforth each is all, in God. There is no higher, no deeper, no other than the life in which we are founded. "The One remains, the many change and pass." And each and every of us is the One that remains. Listen, then to the charming of the Prince of Peace, who takes away the sin from the world, and say, each for himself, "My father and I are one." Mourn not for the dead, who have awoke in the bosom of God. They care not, they think not, and when we are what they are, we too shall think of them no more. Much might I say of the good of this discovery, if it were, as it soon may be, generally known of. Now for the first time, the ancient problem is referred to empirical resolution, when the expert and the novice may meet equally on the same ground. My worldly tribulation reclines on its divine composure; and though not in

74

haste to die, I "care not to be dead," but look into the future with serene and changeless cheer. This world is no more than that alien terror which was taught me. Spurning the cloud-grimed and still sultry battlements whence so lately Jehovan thunders boomed, my gray gull lifts her wing against the nightfall, and takes the dim leagues with a fearless eye.

By this revelation we enter to the sadness and majesty of Jesus -- to the solemn mystery which inspired the prophets of every generation. By some accident of being they entered into this condition. This is "the voice of One crying in the wilderness, Make straight the way of the Lord: 'He that hath ears to hear let him hear. Heed not for themselves the voice nor the hand, which ever deny themselves; remember only how many inspired times it is spoken and written: I AM -- that God whom faltering spirits seek in far-off courts of Heaven, while behold! the kingdom of God is neither lo! here nor lo! there but within you; it is the Soul. Thou shalt vanish, but the soul is eternal: I speak not of souls. And behold, I say unto you, the Supreme Genius does not factualize; the glory is not what it does but what it is; it hath no old nor new, no here nor there; it stays not to remember, to wonder, to compare; to the whim of the patrician Presence, omniscience were an idle labor and delay, and prophecy is forestalled and bootless in the sole sufficiency whose paean hath no echo.

This is the Ultimatum. It is no glance between conditions, as if in passing from this sphere of existence we might catch a glimpse of

> the Gods, who haunt
> the lucid interspace of world and world,
> Where never creeps a cloud, or moves a wind
> Nor ever falls the least white star of snow.

and lose them again as we pass onto another orb and organization. This thick net of space containing all worlds -- this fate of being which contains both gods and men, is the capacity of the Soul, and can be claimed as greater than us only by claiming a greater than the greatest, and denying God and safety. As sure as being -- whence is all our care -- so sure is content, beyond duplexity, antithesis, or trouble, where I have triumphed in a solitude that God is not above.

It is written that "there was war in heaven," that aeons of dominion, as absolute as any, beheld the banners of Lucifer streaking with silver and crimson the mists of the morning, and heard the heavy guns of Moloch and Belial beating on the heights of the mind; and I read that dead men have appeared as human forms; -- nought of this can I deny, more or better than I can deny myself. The tales, whether they be true or false; are as substantial as the things of which they tell.

> "We are such stuff
> As dreams are made of, and our little life
> Is rounded with a sleep."

73

*   *   *   *

In **The Varieties of Religious Experience,** William James quotes from Benjamin Paul Blood's *"Tennyson's Trances and the Anesthetic Revelation,"* which James referred to as "Blood's latest pamphlet" (**Varieties of Religious Experience,** Published: 1902).

"The Anesthetic Revelation is the Initiation of Man into the Immemorial Mystery of the Open Secret of Being, revealed as the Inevitable Vortex of Continuity. Inevitable is the word. Its motive is inherent -- it is what has to be. It is not for any love or hate, nor for joy nor sorrow, nor good nor ill. End, beginning, or purpose, it knows not of.

"It affords no particular of the multiplicity and variety of things; but it fills appreciation of the historical and the sacred with a secular and intimately personal illumination of the nature and motive of existence, which then seems reminiscent -- as if it should have appeared, or shall yet appear, to every participant thereof.

"Although it is at first startling in its solemnity, it becomes directly such a matter of course -- so old fashioned, and so akin to proverbs, that it inspires exultation rather than fear, and a sense of safety, as identified with the aboriginal and the universal. But no words may express the imposing certainty of the patient that he is realizing the primordial, Adamic surprise of Life.

"Repetition of the experience finds it ever the same, and as if it could not possibly be otherwise. The subject resumes his normal consciousness only to partially and fitfully remember its occurrence, and to try to formulate its baffling import, -- with only this consolatory after thought: that he has known the oldest truth, and that he has done with human theories as to the origin, meaning or destiny of the race. He is beyond instruction in 'spiritual things'.

"The lesson is one of central safety: the Kingdom is within. All days are judgment days: but there can be no climacteric purpose of eternity, nor any scheme of the whole. The astronomer abridges the row of bewildering figures by increasing his unit of measurement: so we may reduce the distracting multiplicity of things to the unity for which each of us stands.

"This has been my moral sustenance since I have known of it. In my first printed mention of it I declared: 'The world is no more the alien terror that was taught me. Spurning the cloud-grimed and still sultry battlements whence so lately Jehovan thunders boomed, my gray gull lifts her wing against the nightfall, and takes the dim leagues with a fearless eye.' And now, after twenty-seven years of this experience, the wing is grayer, but the eye is fearless still, while I renew and doubly emphasize that declaration. I know -- as having known -- the meaning of Existence: the sane centre of the universe -- at once the wonder and the assurance of the soul -- for which the speech of reason has as yet no name but the Anesthetic Revelation."

(James considerably abridged the quotation.)

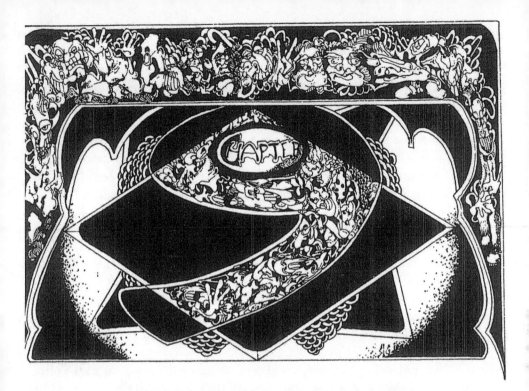

SUBJECTIVE EFFECTS OF NITROUS OXIDE

by William James

Reprinted from "Mind", Vol. 7, 1882, pp. 186 - 208.

Some observations of the effects of nitrous oxide gas-intoxication which I was prompted to make by reading the pamphlet called *"The anaesthetic revelation and the gist of philosophy"* (Blood, 1874), have made me understand better than ever before both the strength and the weakness of Hegel's philosophy. I strongly urge others to repeat the experiment, which with pure gas is short and harmless enough. The effects will of course vary with the individual, just as they vary in the same individual from time to time; but it is probable that in the former case, as in the latter, a generic resemblance will obtain. With me, as with every other person of whom I have heard, the keynote of the experience is the tremendously exciting sense of an intense metaphysical illumination. Truth lies open to the view in depth beneath depth of almost blinding evidence. The mind sees all the logical relations of being with an apparent subtlety and instantaniety to which its normal consciousness offers no parallel; only as sobriety returns, the feeling of insight fades, and one is left staring vacantly at a few disjointed words and phrases, as one stares at a cadaverous-looking snow-peak from which the sunset glow has just fled, or at the black cinder left by an extinguished brand.

The immense emotional sense of reconciliation which characterizes the "maudlin" stage of alcoholic drunkenness -- a stage which seems silly to lookers-on, but the subjective rapture of which probably constitutes a chief part of the temptation to the vice -- is well known. The centre and periphery of things seem to come together. The ego and its objects, the meum and the tuum, are one.

Now this, only a thousandfold enhanced, was the effect upon me of the gas: and its first result was to make peal through me with unutterable power the conviction that Hegelism was true after all, and that the deepest convictions of my intellect hitherto were wrong. Whatever the idea of representation occurred to the mind was seized by the same logical forceps, and served to illustrate the same truth; and that truth was that every opposition, among whatsoever things, vanishes in a higher unity in which it is based; that all contradictions, so-called, are of a common kind; that unbroken continuity is of the essence of being; and that we are literally in the midst of an infinite, to perceive the existence of which is the utmost we can attain. Without the same as a basis, how could strife occur? Strife presupposes something to be striven about; and in this common topic, the same for both parties, the differences merge. From the hardest contradiction to the tenderest diversity of verbiage differences evaporate; yes and no agree at least in being assertions; a denial of a statement is but another mode of stating the same, contradictions can only occur of the same thing -- all opinions are thus synonyms, are synonymous, are the same. But the same phrase by difference of emphasis is two; and here again difference and no-difference merge in one.

It is impossible to convey an idea of the torrential character of the identification of opposites as it streams through the mind in this experience. I have sheet after sheet of phrases dictated or written during the intoxication, which to the sober reader seem meaningless drivel, but which at the moment of transcribing were fused in the fire of infinite rationality. God and devil, good and evil, life and death, I and thou, sober and drunk, matter and form, black and white, quantity and quality, shiver of ecstasy and shudder of horror, vomiting and swallowing, inspiration and expiration, fate and reason, great and small, extent and intent, joke and earnest, tragic and comic, and fifty other contrasts figure in these pages in the same monotonous way. The mind saw how each term belonged to its contrast through a knife-edge moment of transition which it effected, and which, perennial and eternal, was the nunc stans of life. The thought of mutual implication of the parts in the bare form of a judgment of opposition as "nothing -- but," "no more -- than," "Only -- if,", etc. produced a perfect delirium of theoretic rapture. And at last, when definite ideas to work on came slowly, the mind went through the mere form of recognizing sameness in identity by contrasting the same word with itself, differently emphasized, or shorn of its initial letter. Let me transcribe a few sentences:

What's mistake but a kind of take?
What's nausea but a kind of -usea?
Sober, drunk, -unk, astonishment.
Everything can become the subject of criticism -- how criticise
without something to criticise?
Agreement -- disagreement!!
Emotion--motion!!!

78

DR. WILLIAM JAMES , the physician, psychologist, and philosopher was an enthusiastic advocate of nitrous oxide, and one of the few writers to respond favorably to the publication of Benjamin Paul Blood's "The Anesthetic Revelation" (1874). James, in the *Varieties of Religious Experience,* discusses the significance of the laughing gas experience: "One conclusion was forced upon my mind . . . and my impression of its truth has ever since remained unshaken. It is that our normal, waking consciousness, rational consciousness as we call it, is but one special type of consciousness, whilst all about it, parted from it by the flimsiest of screens, there lie potential forms of consciousness entirely different. . . . No account of the universe in its totality can be final which leaves these other forms of consciousness quite disregarded." James called the nitrous oxide experience a "delirium of theoretic rapture."

By God, how that hurts By God, how it doesn't hurt! Reconciliation of two extremes.

By George, nothing but othing!

That sounds like nonsense, but it is pure onsense!

Thought deeper than speech....!

Medical school; divinity school, school! SCHOOL! Oh my God, oh God; oh God!

The most coherent and articulate sentence which came was this:

There are no differences but differences of degree between different degrees of difference and no difference.

But now comes the reverse of the medal. What is the principle of unity in all this monotonous rain of instances? Although I did not see it at first, I soon found that it was in each case nothing but the abstract genus of which the conflicting terms were opposite species. In other words, although the flood of ontologic emotion was Hegelian through and through, the ground for it was nothing but the world-old principle that things are the same only so far and no farther than they are the same, or partake of a common nature -- the principle that Hegel most tramples under foot. At the same time the rapture of beholding a process that was infinite, changed (as the nature of the infinitude was realized by the mind) into the sense of a dreadful and ineluctable fate, with whose magnitude every finite effort is incommensurable and in the light of which whatever happens is indifferent. This instantaneous revulsion of mood from rapture to horror is, perhaps, the strongest emotion I have ever experienced. I got it repeatedly when the inhalation was continued long enough to produce incipient nausea; and I cannot but regard it as the normal and inevitable outcome of the intoxication, if sufficiently prolonged. A pessimistic fatalism, depth within depth of impotence and indifference, reason and silliness united, not in a higher synthesia, but in the fact that whichever you choose it is all one -- this is the upshot of a revelation that began so rosy bright.

Even when the process stops short of this ultimatum, the reader will have noticed from the phrases quoted how often it ends by losing the clue. Something "fades", "escapes"; and the feeling of insight is changed into an intense one of bewilderment, puzzle, confusion, astonishment: I know no more singular sensation than this intense bewilderment, with nothing particular left to be bewildered at save the bewilderment itself. It seems, indeed, a causa sui, or "spirit become its own object."

My conclusion is that the togetherness of things in a common world, the law of sharing, of which I have said so much, may, when perceived, engender a very powerful emotion; that Hegel was so unusually susceptible to this emotion; throughout his life that its gratification became his supreme end, and made him tolerably unscrupulous as to means he employed; that indifferentism is the true

80

outcome of every view of the world which makes infinity and continuity to be its essence, and that pessimistic or optimistic attitudes pertain to the more accidental subjectivity of the moment; finally, that the identification of contradictories, so far from being the self-developing process which Hegel supposes, is really a self-consuming process, passing from the less to the more abstract, and terminating either in a laugh at the ultimate nothingness, or in a mood of vertiginous amazement at a meaningless infinity.

MOSES THOMAS ON LAUGHING GAS (1814)

From: A Cursory Glimpse of the State of the Nation, on the Twenty-Second of February, 1814, being the Eighty-First Anniversary of the Birth of Washington; or a Physico-Politico-Theologico, Lucubration upon the Wonderful Properties of Nitrous Oxide, or the Newly Discovered Exhilarating Gas, in its effects upon the Human Mind, and Body; as they were exhibited, by actual experiment; on the evening of the twenty-third instant.
Slightly Abridged

    The following Paper upon the State Of The Nation, was written and put to press -- upon the spur of the occasion, in the abstract, allegorical manner, of the Tatlers, Spectators, and Guardians, of the last century; which are said to have had so great an effect upon public sentiment, in those unsettled times, as to have contributed, more than anything else, to the prevalence of independent principles, and the quiet establishment of the Hanoverian family upon the vacant throne of the house of Stuart. But the intended conclusion has since assumed a more declamatory tone; which the critical reader is requested to excuse, as the apparent incongruity cannot now be corrected.

Non fumum ex fulgore, sed ex fumo dare lucem
Cogitat, ut speciosa dehinc miracula promat.
--Horace.

One with a flash begins, and ends in smoke;
The other out of smoke brings glorious light,
And (without raising expectation high)
Surprizes us with dazzling miracles.
--Roscommon.

The air of our atmosphere, it is well known to all persons acquainted with chemistry, consists of oxygen, and nitrogen, in the proportions of about twenty-one parts of the former to seventy-nine parts of the latter. It is highly probable that in the atmosphere, the two gases are not chemically combined; but exist, in a state of simple mixture, as when artificially mixed, in the above proportions, they exhibit all the general properties of atmospheric air. There are however three articles, differing essentially from each other, which consist of oxygen, and hydrogen, in a state of chemical combination. These are nitric acid, nitric oxide, (nitrous air,) and nitrous oxide. The latter of these is always produced by the decomposition of the former, and is always, it is believed, an artificial production, as its natural formation has never been observed. --Nitric acid appears to be composed of about seventy parts of oxygen, combined with about thirty parts of nitrogen; nitric oxide of about thirty-seven parts of oxygen, and sixty-three of hydrogen. To procure nitrous oxide we must employ an agent, which will deprive nitric oxide of oxygen, or supply it with nitrogen, so as to bring the exact proportions, the articles of which it is composed; and present them to each other, under circumstances which will induce their combination. This is readily effected by the decomposition of nitrate of ammonia. When this salt is submitted to a proper degree of heat (about 400 degrees of Fahrenheit) it is slowly decomposed; the hydrogen of ammonia unites to a portion of the oxygen of the nitric acid, and forms water, whilst the remaining oxygen of the acid, with its nitrogen, combines with the nitrogen of the ammonia, and forms nitrous oxide; which, existing in the gaseous form, may be collected in proper vessels.

In the preparation of nitrous oxide, there are two circumstances of essential importance to the obtaining of it, in a state of purity. Nitric acid, as it is found in commerce, is always contaminated with muriatic acid, of this it must be deprived, or a portion of a very deleterious gas (oxy muriatic acid) will be intermixed with the nitrous oxide.

Nitrous oxide supports combustion -- a taper placed in it burns with considerable brilliancy -- other combustibles are similarly affected, but its most distinguishing property is, its effect upon the human system when inhaled by the mouth -- an effect so singular, and so powerful, that it is still witnessed with astonishment, even by those who have had the most frequent opportunities of observing it; the exhilarating article being applied to an organ (the lungs) through which no such effect could be apprehended. It is at the same time so delightful, and passes off so suddenly, that it seems more like the effects ascribed to enchantment, than those producible by the intervention of any natural agent.

Passing a leisure moment, the other evening at The Washington hotel in Sixth-street, for the taverns and coffee-houses of the days of Addison and Steele, are with us converted into inns and hotels, and happening to cast my eye over Relf's Philadelphia Gazette, I chanced to observe that Dr. Jones's weekly lecture upon this interesting subject, was advertised for the last time this season. I immediately called for my hat and cane, and sallied forth to procure a ticket, and to inquire for Harmony court, at the corner of which, it seems, the learned doctor exhibits his supernatural experiments.

The lecture room is an oblong of twenty feet by thirty, one end of which is separated from the physical apparatus, by a transverse writing-desk, behind which rise a dozen benches, in regular gradation, the entrance to which is barred across, to prevent the inhalers of the gas from too ready access to the ladies; who are advised, as they enter, to place themselves upon the hindmost seats -- that they may be out of harms way. When the doctor has descanted, at sufficient length, upon the nature and properties of the nitrous oxide; and exhibited a number of unimportant experiments, to which very little attention is paid by his audience, who come rather to see -- than to hear; he begins to perceive the impatience, particularly of the female part of the company, and he proposes to deliver ten or twelve tickets, regularly numbered, to so many young gentlemen who may have a mind to inhale the exhilarating gas. The pit is now cleared for action, and the first on the list, stepping eagerly forward (if he has ever taken it before) receives a large bladder, inflated with the proper portion of nitrous oxide.

On the present occasion the first practitioner was a fine youth of fifteen, who inhaled the gas with spirited avidity -- suddenly threw away the bag, with an air of triumphant disdain, and began to march about the inclosure with theatric strides, until coming close up to the front row, he perceived that one of the persons who sat there held a cane athwart to defend himself from his too near approach. This offended his pride -- he instantly burst into a paroxysm of rage: "That tyrant!" says he, "seized my cane -- deliver it to me! -- this -- instant! -- or -- I'll be the death of you!" At the same moment jumping over the desk, and grappling with the man who had the cane, he overturned everything that stood in his way, and it required the united efforts of four or five men to hold him down, till the effect of the gas ceased, and he turned round to the company with an air of good-humored hilarity.

Several others now trod the stage, in turn, with different degrees of animation, or ferocity, dancing, jumping, kicking, fencing, and occasionally

boxing any one that stood in their way; when a young man of five and twenty
approached the table, inhaled a potent dose of the delicious poison, and began
to display its effects upon his frame, by dashing at the candles -- driving off the
doctor -- and, finally, advancing to the company, he threw himself into the
most haughty attitude he could assume, and exclaimed, with terrifying emphasis,
"By heavens! -- "Twere nobly done! -- To snatch the bridal honours -- from
the blaazing sun !" This violent exertion exhausted the draught he had inhaled.
He turned about as if amazed, and sat quietly down upon a bench that was near
him.

I do not recollect anything more observable, in those that followed, than
that an ingenious boy, after amusing the company by his freakish activity,
turned suddenly to the doctor, and offered him his hand, saying, "Well, doctor,
here I am, at last;" as if he had just come off a journey, and was glad to see his
friends again. Though one sprightly youth danced rapidly round the ring, aim-
ing a kick at one -- giving a slap on the face to another -- and shaking his fist,
at a third; till, finally, throwing himself headlong into the midst of his supposed
enemies, he struggled with them for a moment; and then instantly came to himself, without having spoken a single word throughout the whole pantomime:
for it is observable on this confined theatre, as well as in that of real life, that
the greatest fighters are -- men of few words -- and no pretensions.

A powerful young man of six foot, now offered himself at the table, upon
which most of those who were on the bench below me decamping, I also thought
it most prudent to get out of the way of the first onset, as there was no knowing
how furious it might be. He had by this time inhaled his potion, with the most
evident signs of delight, and was marching, or rather stamping, along the boards,
when he suddenly assumed a fixed posture -- faced the company -- with uplift-
ed hands and eyes exclaimed -- in a voice of thunder -- "Alexander!!!" -- This
exhausted his strength, and as he fell to the floor, like a log, he cried out,
"Lord, deliver us!"

The exhilarating gas was now spent, and I could not but then compare
the theatric rhapsodies to which I had been a witness, to the bombastic ef-
fusions of our western generals on entering Canada -- since the parallel held out
so exactly in their falling away, as the supernatural vigour excited by the in-
flating gas, exhausted itself in fumo, leaving upon the escutcheon of their
offended country, that strain of pusillanimity, which the blood of Lawrence,
and Allen, and Burrows, and so many more of our gallant seamen (the last
relics of the Washington Policy) afterward flowed to wash away: for they have
been truly said to be obliged to fight their way to favour with the present
professedly economical Administration. (Footnote: "If the barbarous and
savage policy of Great Britain be pursued, and the Savages let loose to murder
our citizens, and butcher our women and children, this war will be a war of
extermination. The first stroke of the tomahawk, the first attempt with the
scalping knife, will be the signal of one indiscriminate scene of desolation. No

white man found fighting by the side of an Indian will be taken prisoner; instant destruction will be his lot." (General Hull's proclamation on entering Canada, dated at Sandwich near Detroit, July 12, 1812.)

"Soldiers of the army of the centre. -- The time is at hand when you will cross the stream of Niagara, to conquer Canada, and to secure the peace of the American frontier. You will enter a country which is to be one of the United States.--Come on my Heroes! and when you attack the enemy's batteries, let your rallying word be, The cannon lost at Detroit -- or death." (General Smyth's address to his army previous to entering Canada -- Camp near Buffalo, Nov. 17, 1812.) These military swaggerers, however, have been far outdone by the more ferocious zealots in congress: Mr. Williams, for instance; who (before the declaration of war) wished that he could command the red artillery of Heaven, to drive from her moorings the fast anchored Isle. While Peter B. Porter talked, like an experienced savage, of making a war feast, and spreading a table for the guests. Nay Wright (sometime governor of the highly respectable state of Maryland) and Troup of Georgia, had the treasonable audacity (in defiance of the constitution) to propose to subject their fellow citizens to the operation of Martial Law; and to threaten to have recourse to a Military Conscription, if the ranks of our army -- in the crusade against Canada -- could not otherwise be filled.

But on my return to my chambers, and when I laid myself down to sleep, between sleeping and waking, I carried the comparison further. It appeared to me as though the United States of America, in congress assembled, had inhaled an imprudent portion of the exhilarating gas, which they were now actually breathing forth again -- in defiance of God and man. The gallant youth, who swore that the tyrant had got his cane, and that he would be the death of him, but he would have it again, reminded me of our pertinacious determination to have everything yielded up to us that we contend for. The blustering bravado of the young man that cried,

"'Twere nobly done! --
To snatch the bridal honours from the blazing sun!"

appeared to tally with sufficient exactness to our occasional threats to sweep every sea, and exclude the navy of Great Britain from the ocean. And the pathetic exclamation of him who invoked the name of Alexander, as he was falling to the ground, with utter imbecility, bore too striking an allusion to be mistaken to our flattering prospect of an eventual accomodation, through the friendly interference of the Deliverer of Europe. --

It grieves me to expose the nakedness of my country -- in a state of political intoxication; and I would not -- unnecessarily -- hurt the feelings of the least of her well-meaning public functionaries. -- If I have probed to the quick, the wounds of the daughter of my people, and laid open her bruises, and her putrifying sores; it is not to aggravate -- but to heal: "Faithful are the wounds of a friend." -- [Proverbs xxvii. 6]

86

These apparently "dazzling miracles", however to recur to the motto of my paper, are yet capable of an easy solution, for nothing can be more natural than that the minds of young men, in a state of inconceivable excitation, should turn upon the recollected injuries of their country -- its adventurous expeditions -- or the inspiring prospects of its returning prosperity. Yet the probability of this singular chain of historical coincidences may well be doubted by others: for I can now scarcely credit my own recollection of it. The whole story, I well know, will be supposed to be nothing more than a waking dream, a political vision: but I have only to refer the sceptic to any one of more than a hundred persons, of both sexes, who were present at the exhibition I have described, for proof that the facts occurred, and that too, in the very order in which I have related them, on the identical evening of the 23rd of February.

But the most important circumstance, in a moral point of view attending this singular, and highly interesting display of the effect of the nitrous oxide, upon the human mind and body, is the proof it affords of the exact proportions, in He who weighs the mountains in scales, and the hills as in a balance, has allotted the component parts of atmospheric air (twenty-one parts of oxygen, to seventy-nine parts of nitrogen) -- inasmuch as it indicates how materially we are acted upon by external circumstances, in this corporeal state of being; and how immediately we depend, even for the sober use of every faculty we possess, upon the strictly tempered air we breathe! Is there a rational being so fool-hardy as to attribute this harmonious coincidence between the composition of the atmosphere, and the lungs of the animal creation, to the operation of chance? I have too high an opinion of the common sense of mankind to believe that there is a single one upon the face of the earth.

I mention not this opinion with any view to the conviction of professed atheism (if any such thing there be) for it has always appeared to me, when I have met with abstruse reasonings, intended for this purpose, that it was beating the air, or skirmishing with a phantom. For, whatever some may think, in this age of freedom and infidelity, of the doctrine, truly inconceivable as it is to human apprehension, of a particular Providence (about our bed, and about our paths) or the mystery of regeneration to eternal life, through the medium of an incarnate Saviour, (in which I most humbly and reverently believe) it is only the fool, that hath said in his heart "There is no God."

If art to form, and counsel to conduct,
And that with far greater than human skill,
Resides not in each block -- a Godhead reigns --
"Has matter more than motion? has it thought,
Judgment, and genius? Is it deeply learn'd

In mathematics? Has it fram'd such laws,
Which but to guess a Newton made immortal? --
If so, how each sage atom laughs at me,
Who think a clod inferior to a man!

    I know that I am addressing a moral and religious people, who, like my-self, (though under different names and forms), "Believe (according to that called the Apostle's Creed, which I shall repeat for the benefit of some of those now in authority, who seem to have lost sight of the righteousness which exalteth a nation, of temperance, and of judgment to come) in God the Father Almighty, Maker of heaven and earth: and in Jesus Christ his only begotten Son, who was conceived by the Holy Ghost, born of the virgin Mary, suffered under Pontius Pilate, was crucified, dead, and buried: the third day he rose again from the dead, he ascended into heaven, and sitteth on the right hand of God the Father; from whence he shall come to judge the quick and the dead."

    It may be thought strange to urge the influence of religious principles upon national policy (tho' it is certainly more strange that it should be thought so in a Christian country) yet does Lord Liverpool, the British premier, think proper to avow the supremacy of the moral principle, even in affairs of state. "God forbid, my lords," says he (in the debate which took place in the upper house, on the answer to the prince regent's speech of the fourth of November) "that I should mean to exclude from our policy principles of justice and morality." These are not the words of a tyrant, addressed to the pretended representatives of a nation of slaves -- *vox, et ptaetera nihil* -- like the post-antedated repeal of the Berlin and Milan decrees. They are sentiments of truth and honour -- pledged for actual observance before the high-minded aristocracy of a free and generous people (from whom we have the honour to be descended) and who, like ourselves, have spirit enough, and virtue enough to insist upon the redemption of the pledge, should Administration be disposed to prevaricate.

    In strict conformity to these dignified professions was the late overture for peace, instituted by Lord Castlereagh, the Minister for Foreign Affairs -- the most direct proposals, for which desirable purpose, were sullenly rejected by our present administration, for those which are least so; and a mission to Gottenburgh (an inconvenient, and, in winter season, almost inaccessible port-town, at the entrance of the Baltic) preferred to an immediate negotiation at London; which might have prevented all occasion for the fruitless waste of blood and treasure, which will be the consequence of another campaign, it a peace shall have been made in Europe. Peace or no peace, nothing will serve our rulers but another march to Canada. Alas! that we, the people of America (indisputably a moral people in the management of our private concerns, whatever our loving friend Napoleon may insolently say to the contrary) should be outdone by our enemies in acknowledging the obligation of the simple rule of "Doing to others as we would they should do unto us."

> *Our present schemes are too profound,*
> *For Machiavel himself to sound;*
> *And annual taxes must suffice*
> *The current blunders to disguise.*

No negotiation for peace is very likely to end in accomodation, which is not preceded by a cessation of arms; but the fortunate general Armstrong must have another chance for taking Quebec (or taking Boston) at the head of an army of sixty thousand men, whilst the roundabout mission to Gottenburgh is deferring the promised peace --

> *Till his crude schemes in air are lost,*
> *And millions scarce defray the cost.*
> *Great knaves, of old, their power have fenc'd*
> *By places, pensions, bribes, dispens'd;*
> *By these they gloried in success,*
> *And impudently dar'd oppress:*
> *By these despotically they sway'd,*
> *And slaves extoll'd the hand that paid --*
> *Nor parts nor genius were employ'd,*
> *By these alone were realms destroy'd.*

"God forbid!" I repeat the expression (whether the present negotiation shall end in peace or war) our departure as a nation, from the just principles that would bind us as individuals, by whichly adopting the truly savage practice of retaliation; which revenges upon the innocent the sins of the guilty, and is therefore only to be palliated by the usage of the most barbarous ages.

Just say N2O !

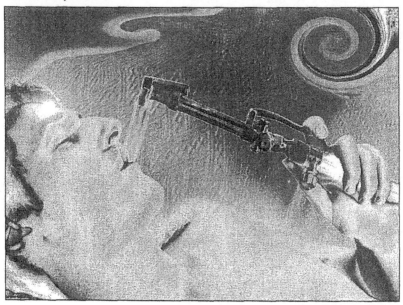

The Magic Wand:
Trigger-valve operated fully adjustable nitrous oxide + oxygen gas mixture
delivery device fashioned from a modified cutting torch.

Chapter 11: NITROUS OXIDE GNOSIS
by Toad

Reprinted from TRIP: The Journal of Psychodelic Culture,
Issue 37, WINTER 2002

When used alone nitrous oxide can be somewhat fun and a generally pleasant experience, but when combined with mushrooms, LSD, or similar psychedelic it becomes a disassociative stargate par excellence. Taking a few hits of nitrous during the peak of a psychedelic experience can bring time nearly to a standstill and reveal inner cycles of the manifesting universe. I'm sure many readers know precisely what I'm talking about as this seems to be a relatively popular practice among psychedelic connoisseurs. Nitrous oxide can also be very useful for shifting gears during a trip and breaking up repetitive thought loops. All in all nitrous is a unique tool with many possible applications for the psychedelic explorer.

Having recently acquired a taste for nitrous along with a plentiful supply I thought it would be wise to do some research before partaking in its pleasures. I was quite familiar with the stories of dentists and habitual users experiencing nerve damage due to vitamin B12 deficiencies caused by the gas, but I really wasn't up to speed on the physiological mechanics involved nor the exact usage parameters.

With the desire to repeat my experiences and experiment further with nitrous I set out to answer a few key questions. How often and for how long can I enjoy the gas without causing any major physical imbalance? What are the pharmacological mechanics of its actions and what are the possible repercussions? Are there any adjuncts or supplements that can be used to lessen the detrimental aspects of the gas? In this article I will present some pertinent data points uncovered from the medical literature that will allow readers to form a more educated opinion.

So let's get right down to business and dig into the dark side of nitrous oxide. It's well known that prolonged exposure to nitrous oxide can cause adverse effects in the blood, nervous, and reproductive systems of humans. Pernitious anemia may become evident along with signs of impaired nerve function such as numbness, tingling and burning sensations in the extremities. Depression and impaired mental function may also occur. Other symptoms can include paleness, fatigue, shortness of breath, diarrhea, and heart and nervous system disorders. One of the most serious side effects of nitrous is that it can interfere with DNA synthesis. This effect has been observed with nitrous oxide exposures of as little as a 2 hours. (Amos RJ. 1982; Nunn JF. 1986).

The various side effects and nerve degeneration caused by excessive use of nitrous is very similar to what is seen with vitamin B12 deficiencies. This is because nitrous oxide effectively dysrupts the metabolic pathway of vitamin B12 in the body. To understand the mechanics of this process one first has to know a little about the metabolic pathway. Once absorbed into the body Vitamin B12 gets actively bound to the enzyme methionine synthase. The combination compound B12+methionine synthase is the bioavailable form of vitamin B12 that gets utilized by the body for the various metabolic processes.

It has been shown that nitrous oxide irreversibly oxidizes and inactivates the essential enzyme methionine synthase, and thus changes the existing B12+methionine synthase in the body to an unusable form. Once the existing B12+methionine synthase has been deactivated, physical balance can only be restored by absorption of new vitamin B12 and the synthesis of new methionine synthase in the body. Physical balance can't be restored by simply supplementing with additional vitamin B12 because it will not become bioavailable unless the body has enough methionine synthase enzyme to activate it. Just how much of the enzyme gets knocked out is dependent on length and concentration of the nitrous oxide exposure as well as individual sensitivity.

To more fully define the exact rate of methionine synthase inactivation a group of scientists performed a study (Royston & Nunn 1988) on 20 human volunteers who were already scheduled to undergo abdominal surgery. The study required taking 800mg biopsies of the patient's liver at various times during a nitrous oxide exposure. It's interesting to note that most of the research in this field had been previously performed on rodents, and the results of the animal testing could be quite misleading if one tries to extrapolate the data to humans. Rodents are far more sensitive to the enzyme inactivation effects of nitrous. In rats half of their total methionine synthase was inactivated after a 5.4 minute exposure with a 70% nitrous oxide 30% oxygen mixture. Humans proved to be much more resilient, with the average inactivation half time being 46 minutes.

There was considerable variation and personal sensitivity noted in the rate of enzyme inactivation in the patients tested. Some normal enzyme values were found with nitrous exposures up to 75 minutes, while one subject was overly sensitive with an abnormally low value appearing after a 40 minute exposure. This makes it somewhat difficult to predict the exact rate of inactivation and provide a precise estimation of the effects. However it gives us a pretty good indication that single exposures of less than 25 minutes are most likely harmless and probably not inactivating enough methionine synthase to cause a problem. This is certainly not the case with repeated exposures however, and care must be taken to avoid a cumulative effect. There is anecdotal evidence that even very short exposures of 5-10 minutes can cause imbalances if repeated on regular basis.

Another interesting study (Christensen & Guttormsen 1994) can shed some light on how often one should partake in nitrous oxide as well as provide a good strategy for harm reduction through dietary supplementation. In vitro data suggested that supplying additional methionine to cells decreased the initial rate of methionine synthase inactivation caused by nitrous oxide. Methionine is a common amino acid that can be found in your local health food store.

Christensen's study was designed to classify the inactivation and recovery rates of methionine synthase in normal test subjects and compare it with those who received an oral pre-load dose of methionine (100mg/kg) two hours prior to the nitrous oxide exposure. Test subjects all received significant exposures of 75-230 minutes using the standard 70% nitrous oxide 30% oxygen mixture. In the control group of normal test subjects enzyme recovery was characterized by an initial rapid phase of enzyme resynthesis lasting for 2-3 days which then slowed down and only gradually increased over the next week. The enzyme measurements were well below the preoperative levels for more than 8 days after the exposure. Methionine pre-loading didn't effect the rate and extent of enzyme inactivation, however it did significantly enhance the recovery rate. In patients who received the methionine pre-load, enzyme levels were equal to, and in some cases even exceeded the preoperative level within 5-7 days after the exposure.

These results suggest that it would be wise to consume copious amounts (4-8g of depending on your body weight) of methionine plus the usual recommended amounts of vitamin B12 and folinic acid prior to a heavy nitrous session in order to assist the body and shorten the recovery process. This data also suggests that there should be at least a 1-2 week interval between nitrous sessions to allow for complete enzyme recovery.

I would highly recommend that experimenters go to the extra effort and acquire a tank of pure oxygen to mix with their nitrous. Using oxygen mixtures provides a much nicer overall effect and will prevent the possibility of hypoxia (decreased oxygen content in the blood and body tissues). It should be noted that unless the gas is administered with 20% oxygen hypoxia can be induced. In order to achieve a substantial effect from nitrous a 50% or greater concentration must be inhaled. If you were to inhale a mix 50% nitrous and 50% regular air you would still only be receiving 10% oxygen which is not enough. Hypoxia can be quite a serious condition and in some cases may cause irreversible brain damage. Be sure to provide your body all the oxygen it needs while you surf along carefree in hyperspace! I recommend using no less than 30% oxygen for the nitrous mix. Oxygen can be easily and cheaply obtained from your local specialty gas company.

After speaking with a gas company manager I learned that the only difference between the medical grade oxygen and the oxygen used for welding applications is the tank and the price tag. Both are filled from the same pure oxygen tank at the supplier. There is a slight possibility of contamination with a used welding tank, however this can easily be avoided by purchasing a new tank and only filling it with pure oxygen.

Users should also bone up on all the nitrous oxide basics as this article is not meant to be a comprehensive all inclusive review. More information can be found in the Erowid nitrous oxide vault http://www.erowid.org/chemicals/nitrous/nitrous.shtml and the Lyceaum nitrous oxide archives http://leda.lycaeum.org/Chemicals/Nitrous_oxide.388.shtml.

References:

Royston BD, Nunn JF, Weinbren HK, Royston D, Cormack RS. Division of Anesthesia, Clinical Research Centre, Harrow, U.K."Rate of inactivation of human and rodent hepatic methionine synthase by nitrous oxide." Anesthesiology 1988 Feb;68(2):213-6

Christensen B, Guttormsen AB, Schneede J, Riedel B, Refsum H, Svardal A, Ueland PM. Department of Clinical Biology, Bergen, Norway. "Preoperative methionine loading enhances restoration of the cobalamin-dependent enzyme methionine synthase after nitrous oxide anesthesia." Anesthesiology 1994 May;80(5):1046-56

Amos RJ, Amess JAL, Hinds CJ, Mollin DL. "Incidence and pathogenesis of acute megaloblastic bone marrow change in patients receiving intensive care." Lancet 2:835-839, 1982

Nunn JF., Chanarin I, Tanner AG, Owen ERTC. "Megaloblastic bone marrow changes after repeated nitrous oxide anaesthesia. Reversal with folinic acid" Br J Anaesth 58:1469-1470, 1986

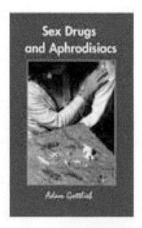